THE Prerequisites
FOR Peace

NORMAN THOMAS

THE Prerequisites FOR Peace

NEW YORK
W·W·NORTON & COMPANY·INC·

TO

generations unborn
whose hope of life depends on peace

Contents

7

Preface

IF A BOOK of this sort needs explanation in a preface, it is a failure. But it may be in order to call the reader's attention to certain difficulties in the way of giving what might be called definitive form to important paragraphs. My whole thesis concerning an American foreign policy intelligently directed toward peace requires comment on current events and on unresolved crises in which no man can predict with absolute accuracy what a week or month or year may bring. Therefore, I ask you to remember that the body of this book has no reference to any development after the third week of November, 1958.

Developments in Europe or the Middle and Far East, or in discussions of stages in disarmament, may within the next few weeks affect my appraisal of certain actors in our momentous drama; they cannot affect my judgment of what has already been done or left undone in pursuit of peace. Progress in establishing the prerequisites of peace may be affected one way or another by what will happen in the next months, but the essential nature of those prerequisites will not be changed.

It only remains in this preface to express my gratitude to a great many writers, thinkers and workers for peace, most of whom I have not quoted or cited by name. My thanks are due to the authors and publishers for permission to quote from the following books: *Agenda for Action* by James P. Warburg (Academy Books); *Russia, the Atom and the West* by George Kennan (Harper); "A Chance to Withdraw Our Troops in Europe" by George Kennan (*Harper's Magazine,* February 1958); *The Arms Race, A Programme for World Disarmament* by Philip Noel-Baker (Stevens and Sons, Ltd.); *World Peace Through World Law* by Grenville Clark and Louis Sohn (Harvard University Press).

I am also indebted for certain quotations and more factual information to the magazines, *The New Yorker, Time, U. S. News and World Report,* and, above all, to *The New York Times.*

A complete list of books, magazine articles, newspaper items, and official documents which have given me information or stimulated my thinking would be difficult to compile, but I should mention my special thanks to Dr. Linus Pauling and his book, *No More War!* (Dodd, Mead), from which I have not quoted directly at any length.

In more personal terms, I should like to thank Professor Charles Price of the University of Pennsylvania for helpful information and, above all, my secretary and associate in the Post War World Council, Stephen Siteman. A rather long illness during much of the time when I was working on the book imposed on him more than secretarial duties in checking material, etc. That same illness added somewhat to the editorial burden on the editor, my friend, Eric Swenson, to whom also my thanks are due for his counsel and help. But rest assured that for what you don't like I only am responsible.

NORMAN THOMAS

THE Prerequisites FOR Peace

I.

The Race to Death

SOMETHING new has happened in the world. It is now possible for the human race to commit collective suicide. It will do just that if it blunders into thermonuclear war, for which it is making frantic preparation. Already the Great Powers have in their possession the weapons, nuclear and biological, utterly to destroy civilization. Survivors of thermonuclear war, if such there are, will envy the dead. That world war might mean annihilation is acknowledged by scientists, rulers, and the people, yet the arms race goes on. It is a race which may end in the peace of universal death. In our bitterly divided world this is a universally admitted fact. But there has been little appropriate reaction to it.

It is the thesis of this book that the logical reaction would lead to a very different policy of war prevention than our own or any other nation is following. The political elements of a logical policy for peace would be universal, controlled disarmament, disengagement from the mutually hostile alliances in which so many nations are involved, and a strengthening of that valuable international organization, the United Nations. The economic element would logically be a cooperative attack on the desperate poverty of a large portion of mankind—a poverty no longer dictated by man's limited mastery of the techniques of abundance. Proposals appropriate to some parts of this program have indeed been the subjects of considerable discussion and a little action, but as a comprehensive whole it has won small attention and smaller support. The reasons for this failure of men and governments to accept the logic of a sound way out of their own fear of disaster go deep in the nature of men and their institutions. They must be examined before we discuss in detail the positive requirements for peace.

War itself as a social condition or institution is very old. Only the family is older. War is a thing which men have at once cherished and hated; the source of infinite woe, yet, for the victors, of glory and honor and profit. From time immemorial it has been the final arbiter of men's disputes. Before its cruel judgments tribes, cities, and nations have perished. But never the race of man. Preparation for war has heretofore been rational in terms of probable victory. Preparations for war may, indeed, have prevented or postponed certain wars. But preparation was for war, not for deterrence of it. And in the end, the nations have always got what they prepared for. For the first time in history, what nations are preparing for now is annihilation.

But even while we admit this truth, so basic has been the role of war in human experience that its changed nature has had no significant effect on the conduct of men and nations. Not only is the deadliness of war admitted but scientists are largely agreed that the radioactivity resulting from necessary tests of nuclear weapons adds measurably to death rates from certain diseases and to genetic peril for posterity. Yet governments have vastly increased the speed and risk of preparation for war over that of pre-atomic times. The quarrels of men and nations have become far more numerous and bitter. The arms race itself has become enormously expensive. Nations in which children cry themselves to sleep for lack of bread make military preparedness the chief item in their budget.

There are economists who say that so affluent is the United States that it and it alone can bear the cost of what the military would regard as adequate preparation without to some extent sacrificing the economic and social interests of its people. Perhaps. But in fact our Congress appropriates with little opposition billions for defense that we cannot match in appropriations for health and education. Moreover, this huge military budget is not viewed as an emergency or temporary expense. An expert panel set up by the Rockefeller Brothers Fund estimates that an expenditure of $46 billion in 1957 must rise to a low of $60 billion or a high of $70 billion by 1967. Indeed in a world in which half the people live on the borderline between hunger and starvation, the anchor of American economy against waves of unemployment has been military expenditure. The Defense Department is by far the biggest business in America. Great numbers of military men, scientists, workers, managers, and profit-takers have so great a stake in the arms race that, consciously or instinctively, they reject the idea of total disarmament. They, and we who are less directly involved, seem unable to contemplate organizing our economy for a more abundant life for mankind as we now organize it for the potential destruction of our race. We ostensibly fought two great wars to destroy militarism and lift its dreadful economic and social weight from mankind. We and our allies won in each of these wars a total victory and are now ourselves engaged in military preparedness of a cost undreamed of by our German enemy. War without nuclear weapons failed us as a guarantor of abiding peace. So we turn for deliverance to hydrogen bombs and nuclear weapons and a draft of our young men such as generations of our ancestors had abhorred. And the nation which with reason we Americans fear was our ally against Hitler.

It would be unfair to describe the world's madness without acknowledging that we are at intervals aware of it. World War II was followed by a constructive effort for peace in the creation of the United Nations, a stronger bulwark, we hoped, than the League of Nations. The UN survives with enough strength to remind us of what rational men might make of it. It cannot now end or even slow our arms race but this disturbs us little because we have accepted balance of terror as a deterrent. We hope that although fear could not make man divest himself of the weapons of annihilation, it may somehow cause him to refrain from using them in war. It is a hope we must later examine.

Meanwhile, men who have made atomic energy their

servant for life or death are about to free themselves from the chains that have bound them to this little earth. In so doing they have already aroused fear that they will use conquest of space mostly to enlarge their powers of mutual destruction. In our technological triumphs there will be no escape from ourselves, even in outer space.

We must prove that our madness is curable. Or else annihilation will end the long, long story of man's life upon earth. Silence will be the final answer to man's striving, with all its shame and all its glory.

II.

Peace by Balance of Terror?

WHAT MAKES World War III most likely is the present fact of the cold war between the Communist bloc of nations and the Western Powers. In this cold war, begun by Stalin, the United States at first felt itself protected from military attack by its monopoly of nuclear power, while the rest of the world was protected by our virtue. After the monopoly was effectively broken by Russian scientific and technological achievements, men's basic hope, such as it was, lay in the prevention of war by balance of terror. Each group of major antagonists, whichever might have temporary advantage in nuclear (and biological?) weapons was undoubtedly capable of retaliation so massive that there could be no victor in a ruined world.

Nevertheless in military circles there seems to linger on both sides some hope of achieving enough superiority in deadliness of offensive weapons and enough defense even against intercontinental ballistic missiles to warrant expectation of victory for the better-prepared power short of mutual destruction. It is probable that some such hope is one factor in the U. S. Army's strenuous objections to the transfer of scientists and facilities now working on the conquest of outer space to the newly constituted civilian authority. Some spokesmen for the Air Force in testifying before Congressional Committees have been quite outspoken in their hopes. Thus Richard E. Horner, Assistant Secretary of the Air Force, told the House Appropriations Committee on March 11, 1958, that moon bases might break the present stalemate of terror between the United States and the USSR if we could be the first to establish a missile base on the moon. On February 25, 1958, Lt. Gen. Donald L. Putt, Chief of Staff (Research and Development) had briefed the House Committee on Armed Services concerning the immense value of a missile base on the moon. As summarized in *I. F. Stone's Weekly,* October 20, 1958, General Putt said that "if we had missile bases on the moon, 'an enemy would have to launch an overwhelming nuclear attack against those bases one to two days prior to attacking the continental United States.' Otherwise the moon bases, observing an attack on the U. S., could retaliate by destroying the attacker. Even if the enemy destroyed us by surprise attack, our moon bases would destroy him. On the other hand, if the enemy attacked our moon bases first to make such retaliation impossible, the attack would be observed from earth and give us warning. Thus the strategy of mutual deterrence would be given a new lunar dimension."

It is fair to add that President Eisenhower is committed to civilian control—if possible, on an international basis—of activities in space. And many scientists have questioned not only the assumed ease of establishing a base on the moon but also its military value. It will be remembered that at the time of the launching of the Pioneer, which went far into outer space although it did not establish an orbit around the moon, the scientists saw to it that the Pioneer was sterilized by ultraviolet rays lest, should it hit the moon, it might contaminate any possible faint beginnings of life on that frozen satellite. It was a caution greater than governments have shown in nuclear tests on earth affecting living human beings. But in the competition of the arms race there can be no doubt that some highly placed American militarists and scientists still dream of recovering an offensive superiority almost equal in value to our former monopoly of A-bombs.

Moreover, from time to time, the public is treated to a statement by some high military authority suggesting that defense even against intercontinental ballistic missiles may yet catch up with the offense. But so destructive are even the less powerful of nuclear bombs and missiles that defense, to be effective, would have to be close to absolute. And no one has dared to dream of such defense in a world in which—to take one example—Senator Kennedy (speech of August 14, 1958) affirms that by 1960 the probable power of submarines in launching missiles under water could destroy 85 percent of our industry, 43 of our 58 largest cities, and most of the world's population. This statement takes no account of what could be done by bombs or missiles launched from land or planes.

The overwhelming weight of informed opinion is that we shall find security against annihilation not in any achievable superiority in any sort of weapons but in balance of terror. However, it is not expected—or even desired—that balance of terror will prevent limited wars which the United States in its own interest or in fulfillment of its role as guardian of the "free world" may be required to fight. Dr. Henry Kissinger has written a kind of bible for believers in this point of view. In his *Nuclear Weapons and Foreign Policy* he is at some pains to refute any notion of adequate defense against thermonuclear weapons which have no inherent upper limits. He believes that we must surely do what is necessary to maintain this stalemate in the deadliest weapons and then, in relative security against annihilation, to develop our capacity to wage limited war.

No one has given a better or more vivid compilation of facts and figures on the destruction inherent in total war than has Dr. Kissinger. He reminds us that a successful attack on the 50 most important American cities containing half the American population would produce 15 to 20 million dead and 20 to 25 million injured. He is especially forceful in showing the near impossibility of caring for the injured; in the vast areas of devastation, organized social life would be destroyed; most of the personnel and facilities of government would perish; panic and horror would grip survivors.

It is difficult to see how this judgment could be greatly

modified were we to build the elaborate underground burrows which from time to time are urged upon us. How
much time should we have to get in them before attack?
And after attack, how would survivors reach them and
how be organized in them? Some scientists have estimated
that to be properly provisioned, these enormously costly
burrows must house at least two years' supply of food and
an abundance of the most necessary types of machinery if
life is to be renewed after the holocaust has passed. Ground,
air, and water would be contaminated for very considerable
lengths of time.

Prof. J. Rotblatt (Charing Cross Hospital, London)
told the recent conference of scientists in Austria—the
third in a series begun at Pugwash in Canada—that he
estimates total stockpiles of from 5,000 to 10,000 H-bombs
already in existence; that 50 dropped on Britain would kill
80 percent of the population; that no one could live in
the open for from one to three years; that no food could
be grown for longer; and finally that if any belligerent
should encase bombs with cobalt and use them in war he
could kill all living beings on earth in three weeks.

Dr. Kissinger first describes total war between con-
testants armed with the most terrible weapons in terms
which would make it madness for any nation to indulge
in it. Then he argues that American foreign policy may
safely contemplate limited war in which some less terrible nuclear weapons may be used. Behind his whole
thesis lie two assumptions stated rather than proved. The
first is that devotion to national sovereignty will make
universal, controlled disarmament under a strengthened

UN impossible; and the second that nations mad enough to go to war or to risk war in the nuclear age will remain sane enough, even when threatened by defeat, to refrain from trying out the weapons which are the secret pride of their makers and owners.

The first assumption, as we shall later contend, is unwarranted, at least until far more persistent, intelligent, and imaginative efforts have been made to bring about disarmament down to a police level under a strengthened UN. The second flies in the face of every reasonable probability. To give it any validity its advocates must assume that wars, big or little, will come only on the relatively rational decision of heads of state, men so masters of themselves and of the instruments they use that they can determine whether any war and, if so, how much war will serve the national interest. How many wars in history have revealed leaders thus able "to ride the whirlwind and guide the storm"? What confidence would Dr. Kissinger have in any of the existing governments once the die is cast for war?

"Limited" wars, short of annihilation, can be bad enough. No American would lightly accept another Korean war. But that, despite the false accusations of the Communists, was fought without the use of germs or atom bombs. Nothing of the sort can be said about another war of comparable magnitude. Americans would inevitably use some nuclear weapons. Increasingly such weapons are becoming part of the conventional armaments of the army, navy, and air force. Certainly they were taken to Lebanon, although the newspapers reported a reluctance on the part of the Defense Department to answer questions on the matter.

The Pentagon used simulated tactical nuclear weapons but not strategic in the war exercises called Exercise Sagebrush held in Louisiana in November 1955. The whole business was over in five weeks. Yet Richard Rovere reported in *The New Yorker* that by military admission, had the weapons been real the destruction of life and property would have been greater than in the Civil War, 1861–1865. Only in contrast to a world war directed toward total annihilation can the suffering inherent in limited wars fought with nuclear weapons be regarded as tolerable.

It is possible but unlikely that the end of our civilization will come by reason of a frontal attack by one of the two great Powers, the Soviet Union or the United States, upon the other. It would come only if one or other Power should conceive that it had a great temporary superiority in weapons. Such war would almost surely be begun by a surprise attack. Efforts to set up machinery to prevent such attack are worthwhile, but to impose Marquis of Queensberry rules on this grim sport would seem harder than disarmament. World War III, however, is far more likely to be the result of what begins as a brushfire war rather than a head-on conflict. The bonds of alliances, Warsaw Pact, NATO, SEATO, Baghdad Pact, etc., would be fuses along which the flames of war would run.

Things would move fast, since retaliation must be almost immediate if it is to be at all. Such protection as our forefathers gave us by reserving to Congress the right to declare war has long been of doubtful value since any

President by his management of foreign policy can create a condition in which Congress has virtually no choice but to declare war. In our era of peace under threat of massive retaliation, our fate is literally in the hands not merely of heads of governments but of hundreds of anonymous colonels—our own, our allies', and our enemies'. As things are now going, it is only a question of time until practically every force of every sizable nation on land, on sea, and in the air, patrolling boundaries, the seas, and the skies, will be armed with nuclear weapons. Many of them will have in custody some of the most dangerous weapons for use in instant retaliation. It was a French colonel, still anonymous to most Americans, not the French government, who almost extended the Algerian war throughout North Africa by his private decision to bomb a Tunisian village, using American planes given France for protection on the European continent. Are there no other colonels among our allies and our enemies, scattered around the world, who might out of anger, fear, crazy dreams of glory or plain error, commit a similar but more costly aggression? As for our own colonels, granting the excellence of the Defense Department's precautions, could no false reading of radar, no accidental explosion in the wrong place of bomb or missile, no mistaken report of attack far away make a commander, perhaps a commander long under tension, release his bombs or missiles in what he thinks is retaliation against the enemy?

It is considered a statistical impossibility to set up an absolutely foolproof protection against accident when controls must be in the hands of fallible men. Our present most powerful guardians, the men of the Air Force, have frequently, although accidentally, strayed over the borders not only of the Soviet Union but of other countries as well —the kind of accident which would very much annoy our own people were Russian military planes to appear over, let us say, Alaska.

Moscow formally charged or suggested that our air patrol constantly maintained in the Arctic carried hydrogen and atomic bombs and that "they may have been sent in the direction of the borders of the Soviet Union as a result of a misinterpreted radar blip or other false alert."

In its reply to that charge, on July 31, 1958, the State Department worded its answer thus: "The Government of the United States gives categorical assurances that the United States has never had the need to launch nor in fact has it ever launched any atomic bomber flight of this type. Furthermore if dependable and adequate safeguards were to be provided against surprise attack, then, of course, any United States flights entering or leaving or operating within an Arctic zone would conform to agreed control measures."

It is indeed a relief to learn that our boys do not, day and night, fly the Arctic with atom bombs at their feet. But what if under some strain the government does "feel a need" to arm its patrol with atomic or hydrogen bombs? And that something slips so that one flyer or many do not get directions to return and hence, under a standing order from that grim patrol, go on to drop their bombs on a Soviet objective? The New York *Times* reported (October

7, 1958) on the authority of General Earle E. Partridge, who heads the North American Air Command, that his command was authorized to fire a nuclear weapon in combat without specific authorization from the President.

It is in precisely such a situation, which one needs no fevered imagination to conjure up, that war may come. And if a limited war is already somewhere under way and tension between the two great Powers is already near the breaking point, it would take far more than relatively cool judgment by heads of states to prevent a disastrous incident or accident, perhaps the blunder of a subordinate, which would negate a president's resolution to keep the war in nice tidy bounds of geographical extent and destructive power.

The danger would be greater because familiarity inevitably dulls the edge of horror which has made scientists and soldiers shrink from the fascinating research into the destructive use of nuclear power and which conceivably would make an enlisted airman or missile dispatcher pause before releasing total destruction not only on an armed enemy force but on the civilian population—men, women, and children. Daniel Lang, writing in *The New Yorker*, comments on the great change of atmosphere which he found among the scientists in Alamogordo on his recent visit, contrasted with his visit four years previously. Their consciences are at rest. They are serving their country. What resistance would they or the men actually fighting a limited war offer to the temptation to end things by trying the ultimate or at any rate almost the ultimate weapon in their possession? And short of those ultimate weapons, how terrible are those other weapons in men's armory: biological, poison gas, and flame throwers!

The concept of peace through balance of terror or nuclear stalemate, becomes greatly complicated as more sovereign nations have the desire and the capacity to produce thermonuclear weapons. Today only Great Britain, our ally, in addition to the Great Powers, the USA and the USSR, has tested and produced thermonuclear weapons. Tomorrow, General De Gaulle has publicly avowed, France will hold her own tests and produce her own weapons. This, regardless of any possible agreement of the three nuclear Powers to end tests unless they will proceed to destroy their existing stockpiles of weapons. It is only a question of time before nation after nation will join the club of potential suicides and each such nation by its passion or blunder may involve mankind in its destruction.

The present British Government, relying on deterrence by thermonuclear arms, has greatly reduced its capacity to wage the limited war for which Dr. Kissinger argues that the free world should prepare. British reaction to the government's policy is worth our notice. There has been widespread recognition that thermonuclear armament may not always deter. We have, then, at one extreme the Archbishop of Canterbury's declaration that his flock must be brave and go fearlessly on, although it may be in God's providence that mankind shall perish in nuclear war. The Archbishop disregards the fact that his view requires those whom he would regard as God's chosen, the redeemed, the followers of Christ, to be active in destroying their fellows by means surpassing in effective horror what their ancestors had attributed to the devil. If this indeed be within God's providence, would not men in dying better assert their essential dignity and decency by cursing God?

At an opposite extreme the Archbishop's fellow churchman, the Bishop of Manchester, declared that it would be better to be defeated than use the hydrogen bomb. There has been some revival of the Christian (or Gandhian) belief that evil can only be overcome by good; that refusal to use violence against violence need not mean surrender to tyranny but choice of a better way—not, to be sure, well-defined in the maze of international politics. The humanist, Bertrand Russell, finds great unrealism in posing to mankind on the verge of extinction the conscious choice of liberty or death. They will not, they should not, choose death which is permanent. Liberty may be rewon. Meanwhile Commander Stephen King-Hall, no pacifist, puts his hope for England on deliberate and publicized nuclear disarmament but with great emphasis on preparation to carry on the sort of civil disobedience or guerrilla war that might paralyze a conqueror. The able political theorist, G. F. Hudson, concerned, like the American, Dr. Kissinger, about the necessity to be ready to fight limited war, affirms that "strategic bombardment" won't be used on a scale of total destruction and therefore cannot be decisive. Mr. Hudson writes: "However vast the destruction that might be inflicted by such means, the decision would be reached by the capacity to destroy the enemy's armed forces and control his territory." * This may be true, but

* *U. S. News and World Report*, July 19, 1957

its truth adds no assurance that in the nuclear age a war once begun can be confined even to such limits of destruction as characterized World War II. Certainly there has been nothing in either the British or the American debate to justify confidence that a stalemate in the most deadly thermonuclear weapons will prevent their use, while making possible the use of less destructive weapons in limited war. On the contrary, increasing emphasis on missiles demands the use of warheads capable of the maximum destruction over the widest possible area.

Perhaps men will wage one or more fairly sizable wars which will not grow to dimensions of annihilation. Annihilation, even if the worst of weapons is used, may not be complete. The radioactive fallout may not be sufficient to make monsters out of the survivors. Perhaps, as Arnold Toynbee and others have suggested, some remote African tribe will be spared, slowly to evolve a new civilization at least no worse than our own.

But what curse is on us that so many men, some of them ministers of religion, are so wedded to the ancient cherished and hated institution of war, so sure of "our" virtue and "their" diabolism, that they dismiss all thought of divesting ourselves of the weapons by which our race can die and insist instead on achieving "security" through intensifying terror!

III.

"You Can't Trust Russia"

NEITHER MAN'S immemorial obsession with war nor his feeble hope that in its most dangerous form it can be avoided by balance of terror can fully explain the popular indifference to, or suspicion of, universal, controlled disarmament under a strengthened United Nations.

In speaking widely across the country on the prerequisites for peace, I have found men pretty well agreed that the logical answer to our fear of the race to death is disarmament and an effort to substitute law for war under a strengthened UN. They may disagree as to how this is to be done, but the great difficulty, the thing that keeps their fear of nuclear war from being constructive, is another fear expressed bluntly and repeatedly: "You can't trust Russia."

By the time of the Czechoslovakia coup, most Americans came to fear and hate our wartime ally, Stalin, as they had scarcely hated Hitler. Khrushchev may have eased that fear but certainly he has not ended it. There is still reason in the record to raise the question, Can we trust Russia? Hence the necessity to begin any discussion of a way to peace better than any H-bomb or missile can provide with an inquiry whether a large section of mankind or its government is so far beyond the human pale that under no circumstances can we trust any sort of agreement with it.

Lenin was indeed committed in theory to a doctrine of inevitable conflict, not, however, on a national basis but ideological: a conflict between Communism and Capitalism and the nations espousing them. He thus expressed it: "The existence of the Soviet Republic side by side with imperialist states for a long time is unthinkable. One or the other must triumph in the end. And before that end supervenes a series of frightful collisions between the Soviet Republic and the bourgeois states will be inevitable." (Lenin quoted by Harry Schwartz, *New York Times Magazine*, August 3, 1958)

Lenin's statement, of course, was made before the age of nuclear weapons. Their advent did not profoundly disturb Stalin—at least outwardly. He professed to believe that his Communist country was immune to destruction by any weapons. Khrushchev, however, is more of a realist. He seems at once to be more aware of the power of these weapons and more hopeful of winning a final nonmilitary conflict. He has said, "You Americans are threatened with a peaceful offensive—peaceful competition." For him Lenin's frightful collisions are "unthinkable in a nuclear age." (Khrushchev quoted by Schwartz, *New York Times Magazine*, August 3, 1958)

But can one trust Khrushchev's concern for peace, or is it another case of Communist duplicity? We are faced by Lenin's own explicit authorization of any means to further Communist ends, and later by Stalin's gross record of broken treaties, and his shocking alliance with Hitler (Hitler broke that devils' pact, not Stalin). The Soviet Union alone gained territory in and through World War II. It turned free nations into its satellites, blockaded Berlin, and supported massive aggression in Korea. Stalin did not join the U. S. in precipitous postwar disarmament. He refused cooperation with the Marshall Plan and contemptuously rejected American proposals for international control of atomic energy. In short, he initiated the cold war. Khrushchev's famous denunciation of Stalin's crimes meant no renunciation of Communism or of the use of cruelty such as he had learned as Stalin's lieutenant; witness the tragedy of Hungary. It would then, seem obvious that "you can't trust Russia" as you would trust a friend.

But what governments can thus be trusted? All sovereign nations act on their understanding of their own national interests and in its service hold themselves above the ordinary law. It was the liberal statesman Cavour who said in 1860, "If we were doing for ourselves what we are doing for Italy we should be great rogues." It has been said that, at least until the dawn of this century, the American government had an unbroken record of broken treaties with the Indians. The basis of hope of any international agreement is not brotherly love but mutuality of interest —in our time, interest in continuing to live. The civil government which we have attained within a sovereign nation does not exist because of that perfect trust of the citizens in one another—which might make communistic anarchy possible—but rather because of lack of it. We citizens agree that it is to our common interest to substitute law for blood feuds and private vengeance; that we all on the average fare better by working together in certain matters under a properly constituted state even where that state is far from perfect and mutual trust of all citizens in one another's virtue far from apparent. It is the extension of relative trust based on mutual interest and expressed through established institutions and agreements on which we must depend even for domestic peace. In its extension abroad lies the hope that it should be possible to work out with Russia a substitute for war. Without it our two nations, perhaps the human race, are doomed.

Let us, then, examine the Russian attitude more closely. All travelers report a deep concern of the Russian people for peace—at least as deep as our own. True, they have even less control than we over the acts of their government, upon which war and peace depend. But no dictator can forever ignore this popular feeling even though he may abuse it, deceive it, or mislead it. Khrushchev isn't ignoring it. He is concerned about the Russian desire for more consumer goods. It is a demand that will grow on what feeds it. It can't be satisfied without cutting military expenditures. The satellites can't be milked for Russia as once they were. Rather they are an expense to Russia. As early as 1951, when Stalin was threatening Yugoslavia, Moshe Pijade, very high in the governing bureaucracy, told me that he thought Stalin would hesitate to use Rus-

sian troops against Tito, but might try to use Hungarians
or Poles against him, in which case he looked for those
satellite forces to mutiny after any check to their progress.
Stalin may have shared Pijade's opinion; he never used
even satellite troops. Moreover he took great care to pose to
the world as a friend of peace. It was his enemies whom
he denounced as warmongers.

Khrushchev, for the first time after World War II,
used Russian troops outside Russia in his outrageous intervention in the Hungarian revolution. But that was a
revolt against what the Communists thought they had won.
It was not an overt use of troops for new conquest. Indeed, it should be observed that in no case was Communism advanced by naked conquest of one country by
the forces of another. (The closest to it was Russian occupation of east Poland while Stalin was allied with Hitler.) First the Communists won a hold among the people.
While Czech, Polish, and Hungarian Communists were
minorities they were resolute minorities able to form governments and hold power backed by the threat, rather
than the active use, of Russian military might. China was
entirely conquered by the Chinese for Communism. There
is little reason to think that Khrushchev believes it necessary or even desirable to advance either Communism as
a movement or Russian imperial power by sheer military
conquest. He may be aware how effective civil resistance
can be in a country united against a foreign foe. The recent
experiences of the French hardly encourage similar Soviet
experiments in imperialism over conquered nations.

Altogether it seems probable that Khrushchev is reluctant to use the vast powers of nuclear and other weapons of mass destruction in his possession. Such reluctance seems indicated by his actions in the recent crises in the Middle and Far East. Even his threats were more restrained than in the Suez crisis of 1956. In any case, he seems no longer under pressure of the old Communist dogma, fear of "capitalist encirclement of the Socialist camp." I am indebted to a manuscript by David S. Anin for the following quotation:

"On April 22, 1958, on the Eighty-eighth Anniversary of Lenin's birthday, Peter Pospelov, a Party secretary who is often identified as a hard-core neo-Stalinist theoretician, declared: '. . . It would be incorrect to speak currently of capitalist encirclement, since the forces of the USSR and the entire Socialist camp, the forces of the Socialist System, have now become so powerful that it is impossible to encircle them and to put them in a position of a besieged fortress in which the USSR had been for over several decades."

Earlier, Khrushchev, interviewed by *Le Figaro* of Paris, said: "We don't know who has encircled whom— whether the capitalist countries have encircled the socialist countries, or vice versa." This remark becomes the more significant when one stops to remember our old fear that the dictator in the Soviet Union would never give up the claim that his country was encircled because that was so powerful a justification of his absolutism and the burdens he put upon his people.

Today the main weapon of Communism, as Allen Dulles, head of the Central Intelligence Agency, has reminded us, is its propaganda campaign, aided, now that Soviet economy is relatively strong, by an impressive program of economic aid to peoples whom it wants to win. In this conflict Russia is clearly not playing the role of a beleaguered fortress.

What isn't so clear is the degree to which Communism in the Soviet Union or China will continue to take upon itself the role of missionary of the revolution to which it was originally dedicated. It is clear enough that Communism in practice is a very different thing than Lenin envisaged during the "ten days that shook the world." It is fascinating to speculate on what he would say if he could rise from his tomb and speak to the faithful. He would learn that they hold that "socialism has already been achieved" in the USSR. But to him that would have meant that the workers were receiving the full product of their toil in a state already withering away as it approached the Communist society in which the golden rule would be "from each man according to his ability, to each according to his need." Nothing of that sort is remotely true in the totalitarian state of Khruschev, a nation whose economy can be fairly described as extreme state capitalism under dictatorship. All powers of the former owning group have been gathered up by what Djilas calls "The New Class," the Communist Party, itself less the master than the servant of the dictatorship which it created. Differences in earned income in the Soviet Union are as great or greater than in the United States, and they are determined not by principle, but by the judgment of the bosses. This economic system, moreover, is the product of a totalitarian state which shows not the slightest sign of withering away. It persists in denying those individual rights which Lenin believed would come to prevail very rapidly once the iniquitous system of private capitalism should be destroyed.

With Communism, as with the great religions, the farther the organizations drift from the maxims and the dreams of their founders, the more vocal their formal insistence on their credal orthodoxy often is. Nevertheless, I have seen enough of Communist propaganda in Asia outside of China to know how greatly it differs in temper and tone from the Communist propaganda in the Western World following World War I. To most of the peoples in the industrially backward nations Communism presents itself as a kind of mystique, acceptance of which will enable them with minimal suffering to achieve the rise in world power and industrial standing which Russia—and now China—is achieving. In the process they are offered the immense emotional satisfaction of thumbing their noses at their former Western masters and exploiters. What is really being sold is a dictatorial, planned social order, avowedly for the people, but not controlled by them. The tremendous debates on economic and political theory which Communists, socialists, liberals, and conservatives carried on in the United States and Western Europe between the wars find scarcely an echo in the countries seeking to rise out of poverty by copying either the Communist nations or the so-called capitalist democracies of the West.

One suspects that in Russia itself the revolutionary ardor of Communism is waning. Khrushchev's denunciation of Stalin's crimes let loose forces which he has not the power, whatever his desire, entirely to force back into the grim restrictions of Stalinism. There was a time when it appeared that Stalin had proved that George Orwell's *1984* was scarcely an exaggeration of what the dictator of a totalitarian state, with all the apparatus of modern science at his disposal, could do to the bodies, minds, and souls of men. Much of the dreadful weight of that fear has been lifted by developments in the USSR, and more strikingly in East Germany, Poland, and Hungary. I am not persuaded of any likelihood of revolution in Russia, but an evolutionary process has begun. The assertion that "you can't trust Russia" too glibly denies possibilities of evolutionary change from which official communism cannot be exempt, however zealously it may proclaim its unchanging devotion to Marxist Leninism. Neither Marx nor Lenin, nor even Stalin, could foresee what nuclear warfare could mean. Certainly it is far more reasonable to assume that Russians, including their dictators, will share our common desire for living than to assume that their talk of coexistence is wholly fraudulent from beginning to end.

Those observers, including Arnold Toynbee, who before World War II assumed that Stalin had become so much of a Russian nationalist that he had lost interest in any worldwide Communist apocalypse badly misunderstood the situation. Yet Moscow's Communist foreign policy in practice has often looked like an extension of the old Russian imperialism, to be dealt with as one deals with ambitious nationalism rather than with a crusading and bigoted religion. In a continuing cold war it is likely that progressively, and perhaps almost unconsciously, the Kremlin will use Communism as the aid to its new imperialism rather than putting itself and its resources behind holy wars, cold or hot, for the establishment of universal Communism as a kind of secular church.

The truth is that the facts of life are steadily diminishing the economic gulf between capitalism and Communism as both are practiced. Neither is true to the theory or the faith of its fathers. Khrushchev has begun a decentralization which in time may modify the rigidities of totalitarian planning. We Americans have been introducing planning and controls into a system which is not socialism but is certainly not the private laissez-faire capitalism of the period before World War I.

It must be admitted that this observation on the narrowing gulf between economies applies to the Soviet Union but not to China. The organization of Chinese peasants into rigorously controlled communes, which are more like ant communities than human and which are operated in the interest of maximum production, exceeds anything of the sort in Russia. Mao's revolutionary rigors have caused the Poles to give thanks that there is a buffer state between Poland and China. Nevertheless, in the light of history and human psychology one may doubt the permanence of this ultra-rigorous form of Communism, especially if Red China is someday to be included in the UN family.

Clark Kerr, President of the University of California and an expert in labor economics and labor-management negotiations, has prophesied that "eventually industrializa-

tion is going to bring about a world wide system. . . . The world wide system will be a pluralistic one, more nearly like our own than the monolithic system of Russia. . . . Eventually, providing we can avoid catastrophe in the meantime, it will come out to be a pretty good society." *
Dr. Kerr's guarded optimism has a sounder foundation than mere wishful thinking.

This evolutionary process will not automatically lead us to arrangements to avoid catastrophe, but it can help in the process. Already the Kremlin's version of the original Communist aspirations for world domination is being somewhat modified by erosion of Marxist-Leninist-Stalinist ideology, and more obviously by a growing realization that in the nuclear age, neither side in the present cold war can physically dominate the world. The effort would lead to destruction. Hence my strong hope that the Soviet Union —and eventually China—may present to peace negotiators attitudes which are sufficiently like our own to permit a meeting of minds on what is literally a matter of life or death for us all.

True, the Communist bosses have a bad record of broken agreements. But it is not all black. It took eight years to get a peace treaty setting up a demilitarized Austria. But the Soviet Union has kept that treaty even though little Austria bravely gave asylum to thousands of Hungarian refugees.

Since World War II, the Kremlin has not gobbled up

* *Foreign Policy and the Free Society* (The Fund for the Republic) p. 114

little Finland, once part of the Czar's empire. And, as we have previously observed, Khrushchev has not assumed a belligerent role in the Middle or Far Eastern crises.

All this by no means adds up to proof that the USSR, a totalitarian state under a Communist dictatorship, is now ready to negotiate freely and to keep the kind of agreements upon which a secure peace will depend. It is, however, enough to refute the idea that it is useless to try harder, more consistently and more imaginatively than we have to obtain agreements necessary for peace.

The great stumbling block today is not a Soviet plan to wage all-out aggressive war. It is in the opinion of many who have talked with him that it is Khrushchev's firm, dogmatic belief that there will come a time when capitalist America, vanquished in productive power, defeated in Asia and Africa by Communist propaganda, will attack its great "socialist" rival. Mao probably shares that belief. It is easy enough to persuade the Russian people that the American bases surrounding them are not truly for defense but for ultimate aggression. This Russian obsession may in time be worn away by evolutionary processes eroding dogma. But the process will require a very different approach to disarmament and peace than our government has shown.

For we Americans on our side are victims of a fixed idea or point of view. It is not derived from a dogmatic equivalent to Leninism but, in large part, from a misguided moralism which insists that the only way to deal with Communism, and the nation under it, is to smother it by military containment. Communism and the actions of Com-

munist governments and the nature of their appeal must
be more discriminately examined and understood. Ap-
proximately one-third of the world's people lives under
Communism. We shall have to find a way to live with them
in a competition of ideas—but not military force—or else
in war we shall die with them. There is no sign anywhere
in Asia or Africa that we can strangle Communism or as-
suredly check its growth by military containment. Are we
ready sincerely and earnestly to try another way? The
best way to refute Lenin's dogmatism is insistently and
sincerely to press for controlled disarmament which would
make aggressive war impossible.

We—most of us—believe that we arm only for legitimate defense of ourselves and "free" nations and will never
take an aggressive role. But under the pressures of a cold
war, can we be sure of ourselves? Rather the question
should be, can we be sure of our policy makers? Can we be
sure of their total trustworthiness and the equally total
untrustworthiness of their—and our opponents?

Philip Noel-Baker in his invaluable and comprehensive book, *The Arms Race and the Case for World Disarmament,* published by Stevens in London, discusses what he
calls "the Moment of Hope: May 10, 1955." On that date
the Russians in the UN Subcommittee on Disarmament accepted previous Western proposals for reduction of the
size of conventional armies and some other matters so completely that the British delegate rejoiced that the Western
"policy of patience" had "now achieved this welcome divi-
dend, and that the proposals [of the West] have now been
largely, and in some cases, entirely, adopted by the Soviet

Union and made into its own proposals." On September 15th, the Western Powers which had previously stalled discussion (probably because of the Geneva Summit Conference in the interval) withdrew their proposals which the Soviet Union had accepted. The Moment of Hope was lost. Mr. Noel-Baker, discussing the reasons for withdrawal, finds them "as unpredictable as the withdrawal itself." The withdrawal convicted the West of the same sort of insincerity or uncertainty in disarmament negotiations of which its representatives commonly accuse its opponents.

There have been further shifts in the months since Mr. Noel-Baker finished his book. But in the whole field of diplomatic approaches to disarmament, there has been no such evidence of total Soviet guilt and folly or total Western virtue and wisdom as to warrant rejection of further efforts for peace because of the complete impossibility of trusting Russia to make or keep any agreement under any sanctions. It is first in order for loyal Americans who perforce must also be world citizens to ask how trustworthy our government and people have shown themselves in working for controlled disarmament.

IV.

But Can We Trust Ourselves?

HOW DEEP has been the understanding of the American government and people of the prerequisites for peace, and how strong their zeal in working for them? How far can we trust ourselves or expect others to trust us, when we talk about disarmament and the more effective use of the UN for peace?

Let us look at our record. It is, indeed, better than Moscow's. We did not initiate the cold war, and we not only carried through the Marshall Plan but contributed greatly to the recovery of our former enemies, Japan and Germany. While we had a monopoly of A-bombs, we proposed international control of nuclear energy, and, later, President Eisenhower pushed through a good plan of Atoms for Peace. But unfortunately there is more to the record.

Once caught up in the cold war we lacked any con-

sistent policy except to counter our enemy and try to beat
him in the arms race. We have tended to drift into a kind
of neo-imperialism to which an editorial in the New York
Times (July 17, 1958) gave classic expression. In discussing our intervention in Lebanon, the editor wrote: "The
United States cannot be one of the world's two great
powers and refuse to act like a great power." To act otherwise "would be to abdicate the role history, our wealth,
and energy have thrust upon us."

It is thus that protagonists of empire have always
talked, and always at the expense, finally, not only of
peace, but of the life of the great powers themselves. If
the mighty nations are to emulate Rome, Carthage, and
their imperial successors in this nuclear age, the result will
be no mere destruction of a modern Rome or Carthage but
of civilization itself, perhaps of mankind.

We profess loyalty to and confidence in the UN. But
we, the people and the government, have shown little interest in concrete plans for strengthening it. President
Eisenhower's use of it in the recent Middle East crisis was
selective. He bypassed it when landing marines in Lebanon
on the very day that the Secretary General reported that
his observers minimized infiltration. But perhaps to evade
Khrushchev's first suggestion of a summit conference, he
became a devotee of the UN and the prerogatives of the
Security Council. It had then become clear that America
still controlled the Council except for the power of the
Soviet veto.

American dominance in the UN, and especially the Security Council, has been due in part to our virtues; in part

to fear of the Soviet (Hungary is not forgotten); and in part to the fact that the composition of the Security Council gives the West four votes and four vetoes, one of them belonging nominally to Nationalist China but actually in terms of power representing the American Seventh Fleet. When the Middle East crisis broke, the one Arab on the Council represented an Iraqi government which disappeared from the face of the earth in twenty-four hours. Two others were Latin Americans whose governments never seriously oppose the United States in the UN no matter how many stones South Americans may have thrown at our Vice President. (I comment further on this in Chapter V in describing a personal experience.)

One of the President's best initiatives was his outspoken plea that human progress in mastery of outer space should be for peace and not for war. But the interpretation given to his policy by the American delegation to the UN in the fall of 1958 scarcely argues intensity or even sincerity in implementation of the President's concern. The first American proposals in the UN met the usual Russian objection that they did not want to consider the peaceful control of outer space, through which they might want to dispatch intercontinental ballistic missiles, except in connection with the American bases which threaten the USSR. In time, Zorin of the Russian delegation made what must have seemed to the Russians a real concession. He agreed to a preparatory commission to study the peaceful controls of outer space pretty much on the American line but proposed a composition of the committee giving what he regarded as equality of representation to the Communist bloc. Mr. Lodge on our behalf proposed what was undoubtedly a more representative committee. He pressed the American resolution to a nominal and unreal victory in the UN in spite of the fact that Mr. Zorin threatened a boycott of the committee. One can blame the Soviet delegation for its attitude without justifying the American rigidity. The control of outer space for peace rather than war or preparation for war will not be decided by a majority vote in the UN. It requires agreement, and the committee named by Mr. Zorin included all the nuclear powers now capable of any sort of exploration in outer space. Clearly if the American concern were primarily for results it might have conceded to the Soviet proposal concerning the composition of the original committee and made substantial progress in the act.

As it is, the American rigidity has awakened suspicion in a great many minds. One does not need to accuse Mr. Dulles or Mr. Lodge of conscious machiavellianism to point out that the course they followed in the UN was what Machiavelli himself might well have advised. The American spokesmen are now on record concerning the overwhelming importance of the control of space for peace. Thus they please men of good will and intelligence. But they have found objections which block any promising beginning of international control. Thus they satisfy our extreme nationalists and the military, who are feverishly working to make us first in control of space. Can we trust ourselves when our passion for peace is so easily thwarted or diverted on procedural matters?

We pride ourselves on integrity but incline to a double

standard of judgment. Illustrations are many. Thus, a news broadcaster one day told us "the Russians are playing the *usual game* [emphasis mine] of complaining that the U. S. is about to give nuclear weapons to its NATO allies." Was it a "game" in the face of the fact that Congress had just given power to the President at his discretion (subject to possible Congressional veto) to give any ally not only information on nuclear weapons, but the weapons, except, for the present, nuclear warheads, which the Americans will keep in convenient bases? A great cry went up when Moscow linked acceptance of negotiation for the neutralization of space with discussion of American bases. Yet if conditions were reversed Washington would do the same thing. If the Russians had tried to establish one base in the Caribbean it would have meant war. We have some 275 bases or installations surrounding the Soviet Union. We depend on bombers stationed near her borders for massive retaliation, while the USSR depends mostly on missiles which travel in space. Hence the difference in our emphasis.

This double standard is most obvious in our American attitude to the tortuous, half-hearted disarmament discussions of recent years. Neither side since 1955 has talked about the complete disarmament which was originally their stated objective. In the early years after World War II it was fairly plain that international control of nuclear energy, which the United States, to its great credit, once proposed, would only work as a step toward, or a part of, general disarmament. But Bernard Baruch in presenting our proposals to the UN only referred to general disarmament in passing. I asked him why not more emphasis on it. "Because," he replied, "of State Department orders. I was in favor of it." As everyone remembers, the USSR vetoed the whole matter.

Our present Secretary of State, John Foster Dulles, when he was a Senator, listened attentively to my presentation to a Senate committee of the case for disarmament down to a police level under a strengthened UN, and told me privately that we couldn't urge that; it was impractical. It was therefore not surprising to me that he virtually torpedoed hope of a really successful beginning of disarmament during the sessions of the UN subcommittee in the summer of 1957. He did so by choosing that time to tie in disarmament with German reunification and insist that the latter should be achieved only if the rearmed country which Hitler once ruled should be free to join NATO. It is easy to imagine what he—and we—would have said had it seemed likely that Germany would join the Warsaw Pact.

Mr. Acheson, like Mr. Dulles, was cool to complete disarmament. The late Senator Brian McMahon of Connecticut once told me this story: Shortly after he had made a speech in the Senate urging disarmament, sweetened by an American offer of economic aid to the world out of the billions saved, he and his wife went to a diplomatic reception. When Mr. McMahon reached Secretary Acheson, the Secretary turned to his own wife and said, "My dear, I want you to meet the most beautiful woman in Washington, but as for her husband, I could hit him over the head with an ax." "Of course," said the Senator, "that was a jest, but I suspected it showed his real feeling about my speech."

In the previous chapter I quoted Mr. Noel-Baker on the "Moment of Hope" when the Russians finally agreed to proposals originally made by the West on the size of armed forces. That Moment of Hope was lost when the West withdrew its own proposals, including limitations of manpower. This, the American spokesmen declared, if adopted by the U. S., would mean the breakup of NATO. Why hadn't they thought of that sooner? To be sure, the Kremlin has done plenty of that kind of shifting. The question is, who can trust whom in this kind of diplomacy? It is by a very different approach that disarmament must be achieved.

Again in the summer of 1957 the West rejected outright the Russian proposal for a first-step, monitored moratorium on nuclear tests. In the spring of 1958 Admiral Strauss told me that the rejection was chiefly due to the uncertainty of means of detecting breakers of the agreement. (Of that, more later.) But the Admiral did not explain why, then, the Americans offered a package proposal, rejected by the Russians, including the same suspension of tests under controls, plus other matters requiring more difficult forms of inspection.

If we are to trust ourselves or expect the world to trust us, it is essential that our great governmental agencies speak to us in complete candor on matters connected with atomic fallout in the use of nuclear weapons in war or the tests of new weapons in peace. The very efficient

Atomic Energy Commission has not adequately met that test.

Dr. Charles Price, director of the John Harrison Laboratory of Chemistry at the University of Pennsylvania and former president of the Federation of American Scientists, presented a well-documented case against the Commission to the Second Arden House Conference on Disarmament.

In brief, he accused it of misleading the people for many years on the subject of maximum permissible concentration of atomic fallout and on the routes by which strontium-90 poisoning from the fallout could enter the human body. He pointed out that the Commission, until after the 1956 election, "repeatedly said that the tests involved no genetic damage. Now by its own 1957 estimate 2500 to 13,000 deformed children will be born every year as a result of genetic damage, even if no further explosions occur." He then discussed what the AEC said was an "inadvertent" report, that a test under a mountain in Nevada had been "undetectable beyond 250 miles." On this report a campaign was waged on the impossibility of detecting breaches of agreement by hidden tests. The AEC did not correct the "inadvertent" statement until Senator Humphrey and others some five months later revealed the fact that the Nevada explosion was detected "by at least twenty United States Coast and Geodetic Survey seismographs in the continental U. S. and even in Alaska 2300 miles away."

The Arden House Report was widely circulated in official Washington. There was no attempt to answer Dr.

Price's statement. It left the inevitable question: How completely can we trust the all-important Atomic Energy Commission as to its candor to us and the peoples of the world in matters vitally affecting them and their posterity?

After President Eisenhower had proposed a conditional suspension of tests, a scientist, Dr. Shields Warren, argued on a television program about as follows: there are harmful results from radiation; they have been exaggerated; they are a small price for the gains in the tests, although now further tests, at least of larger weapons, can safely be discontinued under proper conditions. Asked by Norman Cousins about the morality of our conducting tests which he admitted did some harm to other peoples, notably the Japanese who had earnestly protested them, Dr. Warren calmly held that our national security was still the overriding consideration.

He was scarcely scientific in assuming that the test had been necessary to our security, that there had been no alternative to them, and that the protests of other nations were relatively unimportant. However, my point is that this able American scientist and physician deliberately made his idea of the national interest the dominant consideration, overriding all general moral standards. In this field of patriotic concern the end justified the means, precisely as it did for Lenin when the end was the Communist cause to which he was devoted. Can we trust ourselves, then, on any very different basis than we trust our enemies; that is, mutual interest in continuing to live?

Perhaps we should get farther if opponents of disarmament were more forthright. Not many of them imitate the reformed Trotskyite, James Burnham, in saying (as he said in the *National Review*), that only eggheads are interested in disarmament; red-blooded men want the biggest possible army, navy, airforce, and marine corps. He goes along with them, and his fear is that for their own reasons the Russians really do want disarmament.

Certainly a great many powerful American groups have acquired a vested interest in the arms race. The military in their profession, their prestige, their jobs; the scientists in the funds and facilities given them for research; stockholders and managers of innumerable corporations in the profits derived from dealing with the American Defense Department, the biggest spender in the world; workers for jobs in a system which seems to depend on a bastard Keynesianism requiring arms expenditures to ward off severe depression. Consciously or unconsciously they must rationalize their economic interest in armament with their theoretical stand on disarmament.

I can't recall speaking on disarmament since 1947 or 1948 without being asked; "But can you trust the Russians?" And almost as often I've been asked: "But what about our jobs?" It is easy enough to ask if a country needing schools and homes and hospitals as much as does rich America must spend so many billions on arms to give work to its citizens. One can go farther and point to the job possibilities inherent in lowering the taxes which limit personal consumption, or in using some of our enormous savings to help build up poorer nations, remembering that some 80 cents of every dollar thus appropriated is spent for American goods and machinery. Probably more busi-

nessmen than workers are aware of the inflationary dangers
in our continuing expenditures for defense. Most workers
remember only that it was war which finally took them
out of the great depression and they think it is preparing
for war which keeps them out. What a commentary on
Mr. Galbraith's Affluent Society!

But, despite the element of error or exaggeration in
estimating the adverse effect of disarmament on employ-
ment, it is true that a sudden and great cut in arms expenditures would create much unemployment in certain
lines and distress in areas where relief would not be rapid.
Therefore, programs for disarmament should make provision for re-education of workers, some temporary sub-
sidies, and planned expenditures for useful civilian goods
and services. Can we trust ourselves to do that, or is it
only for war or fear of war that we will accept heavy tax-
ation?

And one final question. There is still a conscience
at work among us, even among the military, which says
that at least we shall not use the worst strategic nuclear
weapons first. Maybe it is more than conscience—perhaps
also a realization that once war with these most dreadful
weapons is started, we may all be finished. But suppose
that in a time of great tension or actual war our military
leaders, rightly or wrongly, are convinced that the enemy
is about to use bombs against us, would they wait or would
they do what already has been suggested, make a "pre-
ventive" use of the H-bomb, defend ourselves by acting
first?

The horror of "pre-nuclear" bombing of cities was so

great that it was considered forbidden in every textbook on international law. But it was used without a qualm as a major instrument of war by all combatants in World War II. At the end of that war, the first A-bombs were used without even a previous warning of their power to destroy two Japanese cities. Great was the terror and loathing. Many people said, "war has become morally and practically unthinkable." As late as the thirteenth anniversary of the Hiroshima bombing the New York *Times* carried Meyer Berger's remarkable interview with Shigeko Niimoto, one of the victims of the bombing who survived. It will become a classic, moving powerfully the hearts of men even in the age of the H-bomb. It will remind them of the feeling which, after Hiroshima and Nagasaki, made men in high places and low temporarily resolve that war, or at any rate, the use of the A-bomb in it, must be abolished. But not for long. After the appearance of the H-bomb, atomic bombs or nuclear weapons of strength approaching that which destroyed Hiroshima were accepted by general staffs of the U. S., Great Britain, and the Soviet Union as tactical or conventional.*

As this is written, despite the President's avowed hope of suspending tests, there is a tremendous effort by the military and some scientists to minimize the danger of delayed radioactive fallout—at least in nuclear-weapons tests. Their consciences are at least as responsive to the demands of their professional interest as are the consciences of cigarette manufacturers to theirs in the matter

---

* The proof of this is effectively marshalled by Philip Noel-Baker in his book, *The Arms Race*.

of increased lung cancer. The question is inescapable. Unless there is some breakthrough on disarmament, can we trust ourselves, to say nothing of our Communist opponents, to use any moral restraint in war?

It is the fashion to regard talk of the abolition of war as utopian. At the least it is less utopian than proposals for the limitation of war, in view of the weapons at men's disposal and their attitude toward their use. Once there should be agreement on the goal of law, not war, and appropriate measures to achieve it for the sake of the life of the race, there would be a climate making for trust which surely cannot exist when the goal is merely limited war, which inevitably invites evasion of limitation for the sake of victory in the essentially immoral business of "organized murder." In that business and the atmosphere surrounding it there is no crime but defeat. Our best hope, indeed our only hope, of developing trust in any arbitrament of conflict other than by war depends upon the conscious rejection of war, not its limitation—a rejection implemented by certain minimal social and institutional arrangements in order that mankind may live. On the record, the United States has not shown an unambiguous devotion to that hope.

V.

Disarmament

THERE IS NO one single, all-embracing prerequisite for peace; no single track will take us to the utopia of a warless world. But the political prerequisites are plain. They are disarmament, disengagement, and a strengthening of the UN. All of them require definition or explanation. All of them in real life are so closely connected that progress in one cannot be securely made without progress in others. For instance, a stronger UN than we now have is a necessity for effective disarmament. But any progress of the nations in intention to disarm and steps toward disarmament will make it easier to build up the UN—not as an abstract fulfillment of the principle of federation, but as an appropriate instrumentality in carrying out the disarmament program on which our lives depend. Similarly, disengagement from the areas of conflict and tension which have drawn the Great Powers into alliances and counter-alliances can be eased when nations seek security in disarmament rather than alliance. Equally it will be true that every abatement of tension, every degree of disengagement of the Great Powers from areas of possible conflict will make easier the achievement of universal disarmament.

Nevertheless, one can scarcely escape from beginning with disarmament when one discusses prerequisites for peace. Consciously or unconsciously one judges the zeal for peace of an individual, a party, or a nation by its attitude toward disarmament.

One still reads or hears the contention that disarmament is logically the result, not the cause, of peace; that the arms race is the expression rather than the cause of the cold war. The statement sounds logical but is open to a double challenge:

(1) Historically the race in arms has been a definite factor in causing war. This was notably true of that stupid and brutal conflict, World War I. After its tragically delayed end, Lloyd George observed that the nations had "stumbled and staggered" into it. They thus stumbled and staggered because their readiness for war gave them no time for second thought. The European continental powers were prepared physically and psychologically by generations of universal military training and service. Britain had no such training but her suspicion was aroused and her temper inflamed by the German challenge to her supremacy on the seas. None other than the British Foreign Minister Lord Grey thought this rivalry a principal cause of the war. Before that war he told the House of Commons that "the naval rivalry was the only obstacle to confidence" between Germany and the United Kingdom. After

the war he wrote, "The enormous growth of armaments, in Europe, the sense of insecurity and fear caused by them —it was these that made war inevitable. This, it seems to me, is the truest reading of history, and the lesson that the present should be learning from the past in the interests of future peace, the warning to be handed on to those who come after us." (*Twenty Five Years,* Vol. I, quoted by Noel-Baker.) Much later, in 1955, M. Jules Moch, French representative on the UN Disarmament Commission, told the UN Assembly that "The Subcommittee had no right to wait, before resuming its progress on the path of disarmament, for a settlement of the most serious political disputes." He was "convinced that they were practically insoluble in an atmosphere of distrust, whereas they would constitute no major problem once included in the general framework of agreement on disarmament." (First Committee, Dec. 6, 1955)

(2) In the climate of the arms race it is peculiarly hard to negotiate any settlement involving the major competitors. Our scientific progress in making war more deadly far outruns our skill in composing our disputes. We are a bit like kindergarten children except that we play with missiles and bombs instead of sand and blocks. The hope is that we may have sense enough to divest ourselves of these deadly toys even while we quarrel over the issues that divide us. Then M. Moch's optimistic prediction of a comparatively easy settlement "in the general framework of disarmament" may have a chance. Even boundary adjustments may be more easily made if and when bound-

aries are unfortified like the boundary between the United States and Canada.

The disarmament that may save mankind from destruction must be complete down to the level of a police force, sufficient only for preserving order in nations and, under the UN, between nations. True, that police level may be hard to define but not anything like as difficult as the attempts to define partial disarmament or what I heard Harold Stassen describe as "controlled semi-disarmament." This, he said, was the objective of the American delegation in London in 1957. Mr. Stassen worked hard for a beginning of it, against, it often seemed, his superiors in Washington, and his allies as well as his opponents in London. So great were the mutual suspicions of advantage inherent in "semi-disarmament" that they were a major cause of failure. If, by a miracle, "semi-disarmament" in nuclear weapons had been achieved on any other terms than as a first step toward the accepted goal of general disarmament, the nations involved would develop talents of evasion and deceit quite comparable to the best achievements of shall we say, the French in making out income-tax returns.

One of the difficulties with any intelligent discussion of disarmament has been the looseness with which the word is used to cover any considerable reduction of arms, no matter how temporary or partial. Historically, it has been these attempts, miscalled "disarmament," which have failed and caused wide pessimism on the whole subject. Many times in question periods after speeches, I have been reminded of the "failure of disarmament" because the Washington Naval Treaty of 1922 did not prevent ultimate Japanese rearming and the attack on Pearl Harbor. Actually, the 1922 treaty was anything but a general agreement for disarmament; it applied only to the naval strength of Britain, the USA, Japan, France, and Italy and only to certain categories of ships for which it set up the famous ratio 5-5-3-1.75-1.75. It was limited to fifteen years, and while it was somewhat extended in duration and categories of ships by the London Treaty of 1930 between the United States, the United Kingdom, and Japan, it had expired several years before World War II. In any case, the treaty never covered the air arm, which worked such havoc at Pearl Harbor.

The Washington Treaty is remembered now as being somehow a retreat on our part in favor of Japan. Actually the English-speaking powers had collectively a 10-3 superiority. At the time of the treaty, however, it was mostly attacked as yielding to parity with Britain at a time when supremacy in naval power which was within our grasp.

Justice Daniel F. Cohalan was quoted in the New York *Times*, December 8, 1921, as saying at a meeting in New York City:

"The English are in as complete possession of the conference as though it were being held in London." He declared that it would continue Great Britain's supremacy on the seas and that any "alliance" with Great Britain by membership in the proposed association of nations or otherwise would be a surrender of the freedom of the United States.

The people who maintain that disarmament—meaning agreed reduction in arms—never has worked forget that the border between the United States and Canada has been completely unfortified since 1817. Nor is it true that peace between the two countries has lasted because there have been no disputes. Following the stalemate of the War of 1812, Britain and America agreed to abolish their navies in the Great Lakes and accordingly sank, sold, or dismantled their ships on Lakes Ontario and Erie, never to replace them. It is the opinion of G. M. Trevelyan, the British historian, that in the ensuing years, often marked by acrimonious disputes, "if there had been armaments there would sometime have been war."

Unfortunately the United States-Canadian example, despite its success, was not contagious. However, in 1905 when Sweden and Norway were peacefully separated, one of the agreements making for the success of the separation and a growth of good will between the two nations was the complete demilitarization of a zone 200 miles long and 20 miles wide—ten on each side of the boundary. That disarmament also worked.

While I have been thinking about this book I have been active in various efforts to stop nuclear tests as a first step in nuclear disarmament. To that subject we shall return. But if I thought that governments or peoples would rest on their oars once the tests were stopped, or even after nuclear disarmament had begun, I should desist

from my labors, so obvious is it that disarmament to be
effective or enduring must be total. "Semi-disarmament,"
to use Stassen's phrase, would invite suspicion, maneuver-
ing for advantage, outright cheating. There would still be
vested interests in arms and their increase. Even reduced
armaments would cost money, and to get the taxpayers
to finance this budgetary burden, it would still be necessary to maintain a climate of fear and hate between the
nations still devoted to war as the final arbiter.

If disarmament is to succeed, its advocates must demand of the governments of the world three things: un-
shaken acceptance of the idea that universal disarmament
is the essential price of escape from the destruction of
nuclear wars; acceptance of an over-all general plan for
disarmament applicable to conventional as well as nuclear
weapons and the military who must use them; and a prompt
beginning of a first step.

At the moment of writing and in the prevailing state
of public opinion, the first step would seem to be a universal end of the nuclear testing without which substantial
increase in weapons and the number of nations using them
would be impossible. There is no time to be lost. Entirely
aside from the health hazard inherent in tests, the more
progress made in nuclear-weapons development and the
greater the number of nations possessing them, the harder
will be any detection of them, or indeed any nuclear disarmament, and the more likely will be the accident or incident which can precipitate nuclear war. None of the three
powers possessing nuclear arms can continue testing or
continue to be indifferent to its inevitable end without in-

viting other nations, allies or enemies, to join the suicide club. If the Russian proposal at London in 1957 for a two-year suspension of tests with inspection had been accepted and honestly worked out, it is very doubtful that De Gaulle would have insisted that France test and produce nuclear weapons.

Much of the current discussion of nuclear tests in its concern over so-called strategic weapons, H-bombs and missile warheads, overlooks the degree to which atomic weapons have become part of conventional army equipment in the U. S. and doubtless the USSR. Such arms accompanied the troops landed in Lebanon in July 1958. Philip Noel-Baker, on the basis of reports of July 1957, thus describes an American "Pentomic" division adapted and equipped for nuclear, chemical and biological war. Such a division "consists of five 'battle groups' each with five companies, comprising among them 13,700 men; all moved by air; ready to start in four hours; armed with powerful automatic small-arms, machine guns and bazookas, five batteries of 4-inch howitzers, and four Honest John rocket launchers; *the rockets have 30-kil. atomic warheads* (*1½ times Hiroshima*). [Italics mine.] It has air-borne television and radar to watch the enemy, and infrared ray equipment to spot troop concentrations at night." This enormously expensive equipment is being widely extended in the American army.

More than that, Congress in the summer of 1958 gave the President discretionary power (subject to a dubious Congressional veto) to give our weapons or blueprints for making them to any or all of our motley collection of more or less trustworthy allies. When one remembers that an anonymous French colonel was able to bomb a Tunisian village with American planes given for the defense of NATO, one has reason to pause before accepting the handout of atomic weapons to other nations. The governments of some of our allies aren't even sure of the loyalty of their own armies, as events proved in France, during one stage of the Algerian crisis, Iraq, and to a less degree in Lebanon.

Very little protection is to be found in the provision that actual atomic warheads will be kept in the control of Americans, presumably those stationed in bases in allied countries. It is a virtual certainty that the Soviet Union will have to follow suit with its allies, even with China, which Moscow has not seemed anxious to supply with atomic weapons. It is axiomatic that as more nations gain atomic weapons, the more difficult will be the policing of any agreement by inspection or otherwise. There is enough danger implicit in the fact that the inevitable, and, on balance, desirable extension of the use of nuclear energy for peace will make it comparatively easy to improvise weapons for war without adding extraordinarily to that danger by beginning with weapons and creating the tensions that their ever wider dispersal makes inevitable.

The best single opportunity for restricting the use of atomic energy solely to peaceful purposes was lost by Moscow's obdurate refusal even to consider constructively the international control of atomic energy which the United States, with a generosity equal to its wisdom, formally proposed while it still had a monopoly of its development. A second chance for achieving some sort of control under more difficult conditions was at least temporarily lost in 1957 when Washington rejected the Russian proposal for cessation of tests under inspection and Moscow rejected the American package proposals.

So the tests went on, Russian in the spring of 1958, American in the Marshall Islands in the summer, British at Christmas Island later in the year then Russian again. Those tests were carried on despite mounting scientific and popular protest based on evidence of their adverse effect on the health of human beings and their posterity. Since the American explosion, not only of a hydrogen bomb (fission-fusion) but a superbomb (fission-fusion-fission) in tests in the Marshall Islands in March 1954, the volume of protests has steadily increased. It has been marked by documents such as Albert Schweitzer's "Declaration of Conscience," the appeal by American scientists, and the great "Petition to the United Nations urging that an International Agreement to stop the Testing of Nuclear Bombs be made now." This last-named document was signed by 9,235 scientists from 49 nations.

Because the radioactive effects of nuclear explosions, both somatic (that is, affecting the bodies of the living with diseases like leukemia and bone cancer) and genetic (that is, affecting the human genes and hence posterity) are delayed in fully manifesting themselves, and because we are affected by natural irradiation and irradiation due to peaceful uses of X-rays, radium, etc., it is impossible for scientists to give absolute statistical statements on the effects of the tests so far carried on. Hence there has been sharp controversy between the protesting scientists and the Atomic Energy Commission and its scientific champions—Dr. Edward Teller, "father of the H-bomb," for instance.

Yet the basic facts about the fallout from nuclear tests and the biological effects of radiation are accepted. There has been some quarrel over the existence of a "threshold" and, if so, its height, below which radiation is completely harmless. For workers subject to some radiation in peaceful employments the International Commission on Radiological Protection in 1934 accepted a Maximum Permissible Dose 14 times higher than that adopted by the AEC in December 1957. Today Maximum Permissible Dose and Maximum Permissible Concentration are not amounts known to be safe but only those that are not causing obvious harm. And there are two ways of looking at statistical estimates: one in cold terms of a tiny percentage of cases of, let us say, leukemia, probably due to radioactive fallout from test explosions, and the other the statement of that percentage in terms of the number who will probably die each year who would not have died but for the tests. This number has been estimated by Professor Harrison Brown of the California Institute of Technology, referring to a study by Professor E. B. Lewis (*Science*, May 1947), at probably 0.5%, or 10,000 individual cases. Admiral Strauss, former chairman of the AEC, might have had difficulty ordering a new series of tests if he could see himself by that act killing before their time a whole city of 10,000 people. As it is he justified himself on the unproved and unlikely assumption that each new test (American, of course) makes it more likely that there will be no war.

For our present purpose the major issue of grave damage by reason of the tests is settled by the unanimous report of the UN Committee of Scientists. It is impressive by its very caution and its avoidance of political issues. What follows are its general conclusions:

"The exposure of mankind to ionizing radiation at present arises mainly from natural sources, from medical and industrial procedures, and from environmental contamination due to nuclear explosions. The industrial, research and medical applications expose only part of the population while natural sources and environmental sources expose the whole population. The artificial sources to which man is exposed during his work in industry and in scientific research are of value in science and technology. Their use is controllable, and exposures can be reduced by perfecting protection and safety techniques. All applications of X-rays and radioactive isotopes used in medicine for diagnostic purposes and for radiation therapy are for the benefit of mankind and can be controlled. Radioactive contamination of the environment resulting from explosions of nuclear weapons constitute a growing increment to world-wide radiation levels. This involves new and largely unknown hazards to present and future populations; these hazards, by their very nature, are beyond the control of the exposed persons. The committee concludes that all steps designed to minimize irradiation of human populations will act to the benefit of human health. Such steps include the avoidance of unnecessary exposure resulting from medical, industrial and other procedures for peaceful uses on the one hand and the cessation of contamination of the environment by explosions of nuclear weapons on the other. The committee is aware that considerations involving effective control of all these sources of radiation involve national and international decisions which lie outside the scope of its work.

"Certain general conclusions emerge clearly from the foregoing part of this report:

"(a) Even the smallest amounts of radiation are liable to cause deleterious genetic, and perhaps also somatic, effects.

"(b) Both natural radiation and radiation from fallout involve the whole world population to a greater or lesser extent, whereas only a fraction of the population receive medical or occupational exposure. However, the irradiation of any groups of people, before and during the reproductive age, will contribute genetic effects to whole populations insofar as the gonads are exposed.

"(c) Because of the delay with which the somatic effects of radiation may appear, and with which its genetic effects may be manifested, the full extent of the damage is not immediately apparent. It is, therefore, important to consider the speed with which levels of exposure could be altered by human action.

"It is clear that medical and occupational exposure, and the testing of nuclear weapons, can be influenced by human action, and that natural radiation and the fallout of radioactive material already injected into the stratosphere, cannot."

The Nobel laureate, Dr. Linus Pauling, has called attention to a problem not dwelt upon in the scientists' report. That is the genetic damage which will be produced by carbon-14 released by tests of fission bombs. The annual rate of damage would be low but carbon-14 has an average life of 8,000 years. On this basis he made some estimates at first challenged but now in general confirmed by the Division of Biology and Medicine of the Atomic Energy Commission in Document WASH-1008, "The Biological Hazard to Man of Carbon-14 from Nuclear Weapons." This document warns that genetic-damage estimates are subject to large uncertainties and should be used in this light. Then, according to Dr. Ralph E. Lapp in a letter to the New York *Times* (November 3, 1958), it "concludes that bomb carbon-14 produced to date [prior to latest Soviet tests] may ultimately involve 100,000 cases of gross physical or mental defect, 380,000 cases of still births and childhood deaths, and 900,000 cases of embryonic and neonatal deaths." It is a fact that even so-called clean bombs produce Carbon-14.

On the UN scientists' report, Dr. Lapp had earlier commented: "While the UN report presents a wealth of data on the global fallout problem attending nuclear tests, the real problem remains untouched—the problem of local fallout following nuclear war. I believe the important task awaiting the UN committee today is a prospectus of the biological consequences of nuclear war." (The New York *Times,* August 11, 1958)

A very few days after the publication of the scientists' report, *Time* magazine, perhaps unwittingly, gave the human meaning of the scientists' report in describing the thirteenth anniversary of Hiroshima Day (August 6th). Its story said in part:

"Said Mayor Watanabe: 'We now view the atom bomb dropped on Hiroshima, no matter for what purpose, as a crime committed against mankind.' And he added: 'We have become frightened.'

"*The Fright.* What was frightening Japan was the sudden sharp rise in leukemia deaths among supposedly uninjured survivors. In the year preceding last week's anniversary, 65 in Hiroshima and atom-bombed Nagasaki died of 'atomic sickness.' In the previous twelve months, the total deaths had been 36; in the year before that, 20. Another statistic was just as chilling: of 32,000 children born in Hiroshima in the past 13 years, nearly one in six was deformed or stillborn. U. S. Dr. George B. Darling of the Atomic Bomb Casualty Commission protests that 'the incidence of abnormal births to parents never exposed to atomic radiation is higher than the layman suspects, and it's understandable that when one of these occurs in a family with a history of radiation exposure, radiation should be blamed.' But Darling concedes: 'We are trying to measure the effect of something new that nobody really understands.'

"For the bomb survivors not yet struck down by atom sickness, the worst damage appears psychological. Many of them try to conceal their identities because they often find themselves shunned. Says one Japanese bitterly: 'People are afraid of us. They think we are going to fall sick and become a burden or contaminate them. We know now how lepers feel.' In a public-opinion poll, 40% of Japanese questioned said they would not marry a bomb survivor; 80% of those who would said they would refuse to have children. But the most gnawing fear of the survivors was expressed by one of them: 'Each morning when I wake up, the nightmare recommences. How do I feel? If I find that I am even the slightest bit tired, then I imagine that the dread onset of "lethargy" has begun.' "

At the time of this anniversary the country which had dropped the bomb on Hiroshima, which is still claiming its victims, was holding very extensive new tests on islands and in an ocean that it does not own. There can be delayed action from the fallout of tests just as surely as from the first A-bomb—itself a bomb of a size now considered small enough to be "conventional."

Advocates of continual tests would say that they are necessary to produce that semantic atrocity, "clean" bombs; that is, bombs capable of enormous destruction but without much delayed fallout. All have some such fallout, since the so-called fission bombs are really fission-fusion or fission-fusion-fission bombs, and fission always produces a fallout. It is worth noting that the rush of tests in Nevada before the October 31 deadline, presumably to

produce "clean" bombs, caused Geiger Counters in Los
Angeles to click so violently as greatly to perturb the people. Even if bombs practically devoid of delayed fallout
are produced, their probable use would be confined to
regions that our military hope soon to occupy. They will
scarcely destroy our stockpile of older bombs. And no one
has suggested that we impart to the Kremlin the secret
of making them. Moreover, under probing by Senator
Anderson, the A. E. C. admitted that existing stockpiles
were being "doctored" to increase local fallouts.

This fantastically deadly race in nuclear weapons
requiring the sacrifice of hecatombs of victims on the altars
of its tests has not gone without some challenge. Public
reaction on the whole has been one of bewildered, fatal-
istic, or belligerent acceptance of human sacrifice as essential to national security but there have been even in
America—and far more emphatically abroad—powerful
protests by certain churches and other organized groups,
as well as by individuals. Norman Cousins, editor of the
Saturday Review, and Clarence Pickett, secretary-emer-
itus of the American Friends Service Committee, organized
an *ad hoc* National Committee for a Sane Nuclear Policy
whose advertisements against the tests, etc., aroused considerable interest and support. Its objective is universal
ending of tests under inspection.

Albert Bigelow, a lieutenant commander in the Navy
during World War II, went beyond words. He, with his
associates, William Huntington, George Willoughby, and
Orion Sherwood, determined to sail their ketch, *Golden
Rule,* into the prescribed area around the Marshall Is-

lands. They were halted by federal injunction as they tried to leave Hawaii. On their first attempt to ignore the injunction they got suspended sentences of 60 days from the court; after violating the injunction they were imprisoned, and all served the 60 days in jail.

About the same time, another vessel, the *Phoenix*, sailing from Hiroshima, actually sailed into the proscribed area around the Marshall Islands and the skipper, Earle Reynolds, was arrested. He was convicted of violating an Atomic Energy Commission regulation on August 26 and one month later sentenced to six months in jail and eighteen months probation. None of the other crew members, including his wife, son Ted, daughter Jessica, and Nick Mikami, a yachtsman from Hiroshima, was arrested.

A less personal and dramatic effort was made by an international group, initiated in the United States, to bring suits in the courts of the three nations which had conducted tests to develop powerful nuclear weapons to enjoin further experiments. The petitioners were Dr. Linus Pauling, Clarence Pickett, Dr. Karl Paul Link, William Bross Lloyd, Dr. Leslie C. Dunn, Mrs. Stephanie May, and Norman Thomas (United States); Dr. Brock Chisholm (Canada); Dr. Bertrand Russell, The Rev. Canon L. John Collins, The Rev. G. Michael Scott, Dame Kathleen Lonsdale (England); Dr. Martin Niemoeller (Germany); Andre Trocme (France); Dr. Toyohiko Kagawa, Hiroaki Nakatani, Takaaki Tsurui, Yaeji Matsushita (Japan). The lawyers were Messrs. Francis Heisler and A. L. Wirin. Legal action was begun in the U. S. District Court in the District of Columbia on the grounds (1) that Congress had not specifically empowered the Atomic Energy Commission to undertake tests involving the use of the Marshall Islands and the closing off of 390,000 sq. mi. of the Pacific to all ordinary uses; and (2) that in any case Congress itself had no constitutional right to adopt legislation thus threatening the lives of those yet unborn.

The case was dismissed in the District Court on the ground that the American petitioners had shown no specific injury suffered by themselves and that aliens had no standing in such proceedings in an American court. This decision is being appealed as I write. So far it has not proved possible even to start suits in the United Kingdom and the USSR.

Many Marshall Islanders through their able spokesman, Dwight Heine, appealed to the Trusteeship Council of the UN, to stop the tests which had caused them great inconvenience, and in a former series, some physical hurt. Messrs. Trevor Thomas, Robert Gilmore, and myself filed independently a petition asking to be heard. That petition was granted, setting something of a precedent in UN procedure. We argued that the United States, holding the islands only under trusteeship from the UN, had no right to use them for tests against the will of their inhabitants and no right to close off so large an area of the ocean to travel and to fishing. The Council heard us and questioned us courteously and some days later defeated 7-4 with 3 abstentions an Indian resolution asking the United States to desist.

Two of the abstainers were representatives of Latin American states whose questions to Mr. Heine and to me had shown great sympathy with our cause. They told the Indian delegate that they abstained because they were ordered by their governments not to vote against the United States government. Many South Americans may on occasion be very critical of Yankee imperialism but in the UN, Latin American governments rather docilely follow the North American lead. Latin American countries usually have a representative on the Security Council. Add to them four permanent members with vetoes—one of them representing America's Formosan satellite—and you will understand why the Soviet attitude toward the Western-dominated Security Council is suspicious and intransigent to a degree that dooms the Council to ineffectiveness as an agency for disarmament or otherwise furthering a constructive peace.

None of these challenges to the American tests in the Marshall Islands aroused much interest or public discussion. It seemed as if the agencies of communication played up, or down, to American apathy. Anyway they did scarcely more than briefly report the bare facts—many newspapers not even that.

Nevertheless, there was enough pressure of public opinion and perhaps of conscience in the Administration to make President Eisenhower abandon the American refusal at London to consider suspension of tests except as part of the American package proposal. The way was cleared for the three nuclear Powers' conference at Geneva in progress as I write when Khrushchev consented to a scientific conference on the feasibility of inspection to detect breaches of agreement on tests. The answer of the scientists was affirmative but they avoided all political issues.

After the completion of the Russian tests in the spring of 1958, Khrushchev announced that his government would conduct no more—unless, perhaps, should the United States and Britain keep on testing. They did, and Khrushchev resumed tests, continuing them even after October 31 when the Geneva Conference began and Britain and America suspended tests—an action which the UN Assembly requested of all three nations.

Neither the original position taken at Geneva by the USSR or by the USA and Great Britain deserved the full support of campaigners for the cessation of tests. Khrushchev's insistence on a pledge of complete cessation before he has made any real commitment to effective inspection casts doubt on his good faith. The Anglo-American insistence that even with inspection there should only be a one-year suspension argues an unnecessary and hurtful caution. With inspection, breaches of agreement can be detected at any time and by such breaches the agreement would be voided and the ugly race begun again. Mere suspension for a period of a year, hardly longer than it would take to plan an elaborate new series, will not impress world opinion; it will make it harder to persuade other nations not to start their own tests; it will delay further steps to disarmament. Both sides will probably modify their positions in conference.

While the conference drags there has been an encouraging response to a petition initiated by the Committee for a Sane Nuclear Policy and signed by a notable group from many nations. It was published as an advertisement with a request that others join them. The petition asked for success in negotiating a complete end of tests, and, as I write, thousands of signatures have been collected in a very few days from the United States alone. They will be presented to the conferees and add to the hope of ultimate success at Geneva—or afterwards.

The importance of ending the tests is, as we have seen, threefold: (1) If tests can be internationally barred, it will be very much more difficult to enlarge the number of nuclear-bomb owners; (2) a serious hazard to our own health and to the quality of our posterity will be no further increased; and (3) an important breakthrough will have been achieved after years of futility in the efforts toward disarmament which have been made in the League of Nations and later the United Nations. The psychological value of such a breakthrough would be enormous, and the successful establishment of relatively simple international machinery for inspection will greatly ease the way to the establishment of further controls for progressive disarmament. However, let me reiterate, nothing is surer than that an inspected end of tests, standing alone, will block no wars and will itself soon be nullified by open repeal or the trickery at which foreign and defense ministries are expert. Any realistic approach to disarmament compels us to go farther. The world will not honestly and effectively renounce nuclear weapons and their use except as part of general disarmament.

I share—I hope—the especial horror that so many of the world's peoples feel over nuclear wars. On August 15

our press reported that Nikita Khrushchev in a letter to
the Brentwood, England, branch of the British Movement
for Nuclear Disarmament repeated his offer to pledge his
country "jointly with the Governments of the United
States and Britain" not to use atomic weapons in any circumstances. Perhaps Mr. Khrushchev wrote in honest
hatred of these weapons. Perhaps he would be willing
to renounce nuclear weapons to emphasize Soviet superiority in land forces and conventional armies. Perhaps he merely seeks some propaganda advantage. In any
case in this nuclear age we, the people, would be we, the
simpletons, if we should trust any government including
our own to keep any such pledge, as long as otherwise the
arms race may continue. (Even Mr. Khrushchev has heretofore tacitly acknowledged that fact by coupling this
pledge with some more realistic steps toward disarmament.) Irrespective of the present motives of present rulers,
the Khrushchev pledge except as part of a determined approach to universal and complete disarmament would be
worth precisely as much or as little as did the solemn
Kellogg-Briand pact outlawing war, to which all nations
acceded while rushing toward World War II.

To go back to the days before Pearl Harbor would
require the United States, the Soviet Union, and Britain
to strip their conventional forces of nuclear weapons. The
mere abolition of H-bombs or superbombs would not
be nuclear disarmament. Genuine nuclear disarmament
would require (1) an end of tests and the effort to develop missiles whose usefulness depends largely on atomic
warheads; (2) a diversion of new nuclear material solely

to works of peace; (3) the dismantling of existing atomic weapons, tactical as well as strategic, and the use of their atomic material in our civil economy; (4) guarantees that existing or prospective airfleets will not be used in improvised nuclear warfare, made possible by the inevitable and desirable development of nuclear energy for the peaceful service of men. For example, radioactive ash from nuclear reaction could be distributed by suicide pilots over enemy country.

No nation will accept another's unsupported word that it has carried out nuclear disarmament. Such difficult forms of inspection and control will be required to guarantee disarmament that an international authority greater than that now possessed or used by the United Nations will have to be evolved.

It is the thesis of this book that men are rational enough to take the steps necessary to prevent nuclear warfare in order that their race may live. But surely they will not take them while maintaining great "conventional" military forces, armed with non-nuclear weapons, old and new, capable of making World War III more terrible than any that has gone before. Only in the atmosphere of acceptance of universal, complete, and controlled disarmament will governments, immemorially amoral in exercising their sovereignty, make and keep in good faith a pledge "never, under any circumstances," to use nuclear weapons in war.

In short, a program for disarmament must deal not only with nuclear weapons, but with biological weapons, flame-throwers, the use of napalm, poison gas, and the strength of armies, navies, and airfleets. There has been little discussion of biological warfare in public or in the sessions of disarmament committees. Nevertheless, in 1954, M. Moch, the able French representative told the Disarmament Subcommittee of the UN that "some forms of bacteriological warfare now already devised are infinitely more dangerous . . . are cheaper to manufacture . . . easier to produce . . . they kill far more people than the atomic bomb and moreover inflict ghastly suffering." M. Moch was not contradicted, but we have had no proposals for the prevention of biological warfare. Inspection (which is a primary sanction for disarmament agreements) in the prevention of biological and some other forms of warfare must be supplemented by other methods of control.

The implementation of agreements affecting total disarmament of all weapons has been discussed very little in the UN or its committees. There have been some proposals for manpower levels—a matter on which, as I have pointed out, the United States reversed itself. But most of the floods of words poured forth have dealt only with the new and dramatic nuclear armament. There has been a general tendency to overlook the suffering and disaster that a third world war, fought with non-nuclear weapons, could bring upon mankind.

Therefore, one must go back to the dreary, unsuccessful but informative rounds of discussion of disarmament between World Wars I and II for suggestions for dealing with many of our most difficult problems. In them a certain ground work was laid in revealing problems and formulating possible solutions which nations really concerned for man's future ought not to ignore.

This history is accurately given by Philip Noel-Baker in his *The Arms Race, A Programme for Disarmament,* which I have previously quoted. It is invaluable in its comprehensive but discriminate use of the history of disarmament discussions and its own constructive suggestions for progress.

From the record of disarmament discussion in the League of Nations as well as of the UN, one thing stands out above all others. We shall never achieve disarmament or make genuine progress toward it until its significance to the very life of our race is accepted. No half-hearted approach to disarmament can ever override our present idolatry of national sovereignty; our aggressive or fearful absorption in the quarrels of the moment; the vested interests of both capital and labor in the profits and jobs provided by enormous defense budgets; the professional pride of the military, and the delight of many scientists in military research which is supported by a jingoistic popular pride in the competitive success of one's own researchers in utilizing the marvelous energy of the atom and the conquest of space for the potential destruction of men.

As we have seen, one of the first steps in a valid program of disarmament should be a universal halt under some sort of international control of military nuclear research as well as of tests. Such research has, indeed, indirectly helped peaceful progress. How often we are reminded that the research which enabled us to destroy Hiroshima and Nagasaki was responsible for the isotopes whose use in medicine is saving more lives than the first A-bomb destroyed! Yet what a terrible commentary on us it is that our willingness to spend time and energy on scientific research is still primarily connected with its military use, its power to destroy. Think what could be done with half of what the Pentagon spends on military research if it were deliberately spent for the purpose of conquering disease; supplying us with both food and energy to replace that which we now derive from impoverished soil and fast-dwindling natural resources; and finding an economically feasible way to desalinize sea-water and pump it to parched lands. To bring this home to men would perhaps be the greatest single contribution to disarmament.

Until we get this overriding concern for humanity and its healthy survival we must expect a repetition of the oft-repeated story of the failure at the last moment of promising plans for steps toward disarmament. I cannot too often insist that until complete disarmament is the goal, every powerful nation and some of the not-so-powerful will be compelled to approach every proposal for partial disarmament from the standpoint of its national advantage and if an agreement is reached, the government and especially the military establishment of each nation concerned will devote a large part of its time, energy and ingenuity in the business of interpreting the agreement to its advantage or evading it altogether.

It is this attitude of mind which has been fundamentally responsible for the failure in former years of proposals in themselves of considerable potential value in achieving stages of disarmament. Take two examples: after World War I there was much talk of qualitative disarmament; that is, reduction or abolition of weapons useful chiefly for offense. Something of the sort combined with limitations on the size of armed forces was imposed on Germany under the Treaty of Versailles. It would only have worked if in a reasonable time it had been generally applied—as it was not.

In the nuclear age it will be harder than ever to apply any principle of qualitative disarmament. Something might be done, must sooner or later be done, to fix maximum limits on armed forces of various nations. Each will claim with some reason that special obligations or conditions geographical and otherwise make the suggestions vis à vis its potential rivals unfair. The United States has already backed away from Russian-suggested limits which it once accepted. Even when it is clearly understood that all national armed forces must be kept to a police level for maintaining internal order, that level will not easily be fixed. But let us say it again, a police level as a governing standard is vastly better and more practicable than a "defense" standard in a partially disarmed world.

Distrust in the mutual good faith of contracting governments is so widespread and so well warranted by history that disarmament, to be universal and effective, must be subject to controls including inspection but going beyond it. How, for instance, can any conceivable inspection determine whether great drug manufacturing concerns are producing biological weapons for germ warfare? One suggestion has been that international representatives be seated on the governing boards, public or private, of great enterprises easily utilized for war despite disarmament agreements. These representatives would have no vote on controls but could be present at all meetings and furnished with all reports. They could then challenge and expose breaches of agreement, preferably in reports to the UN.

It might also be possible, if the nations were in earnest about peace, for the UN to establish what Mr. Noel-Baker calls an International Development Authority to undertake "dangerous activities," which he thus lists: "geographical surveys for uranium and thorium, the mining of these raw materials, the ownership and management of refineries for the reduction of the ores to metal, the manufacture of reactor 'rods,' the ownership of the materials, the sale of the refined metals and of by-products, such as vanadium and radium, the construction and operation of atomic reactors and separation plants, like those at Hanford, Oak Ridge, Capenhurst and Windscale, research on mining methods, power development, nuclear explosives, etc."

There is, of course, already in existence, thanks to American initiative, the International Atomic Energy Agency with headquarters at Vienna, one of whose tasks it is to see that nuclear developments are not used for military ends. Mr. Noel-Baker rightly hails its establishment as "a most important and most favorable change" since 1948. But he points out that "various problems about the working of this Agency will inevitably arise: its relation with Euratom, with the European Nuclear Energy

Agency, and the European Research Centre at Geneva; its control over national atomic industries started under bilateral agreements between various countries and the United States; the part which it will play in the Inspection system to be created by the Disarmament Treaty."

All these problems make it plain that disarmament cannot be the result merely of some sudden emotional rejection of arms, were that conceivable. It requires effective implementation which must be supported by a realization that without universal and controlled disarmament our human race faces probable suicide. To escape that fate is more than worth a change in ancient habits and a sacrifice of national rivalries for power. The disarmament that will serve us may be approached by stages, but always the goal in view must be that of total disarmament in each nation down to a police level. As law is the condition of disarmament and peace within nations, so must law be the condition of effective disarmament and peace between nations. In the UN we have an organization which, properly accepted and strengthened, can be the framer and enforcer of the law which shall supplant war.

It would, therefore, be logical to consider as our next prerequisite for peace the strengthening of the United Nations. But first it will be helpful to examine the disputes which immediately threaten the whole world's peace by reason of the hostile military alliances in which most nations are caught. Progressive disengagement from them is essential to disarmament, to the growth of the UN, and to the substitution of law for war.

VI.

Disengagement—
What It Means

THE WORD *disengagement* is controversial and is not self-defining. It has been used by various writers to cover rather different suggestions concerning practical policies. Let me then define it as I shall use it, first, by saying what disengagement is *not*. It is not a return to isolation or the precepts of George Washington's Farewell Address which for so many generations wisely guided our policy. The general growth of the interdependence of mankind, the extraordinary share of the world's wealth and power which America holds, and her role in two world wars make that impossible.

Neither should disengagement be a cover for withdrawal from the United Nations. Rather the contrary. Action in and through a strengthened United Nations is the best—in some cases the only—way out of the various military commitments which today do far more to threaten our own security and the world's peace than to guarantee them.

Disengagement does not mean an end of a worldwide struggle against dictatorship and oppression. It could make more effective our use of other methods than military, methods more in accord with our ends. Going hand in hand with progressive disarmament, it could smooth the road for victories of justice and freedom in lands cursed by their present denial.

Finally, disengagement does not mean rejection of our moral obligation as the world's richest nation to take active and cooperative part in that war against poverty which is the outstanding holy war of our times—a war not to be fought or won with the nuclear or conventional weapons which cost us all so dear.

As I shall discuss it, disengagement means: (1) A phased withdrawal of armed forces from a defined area to create a militarily neutralized belt or zone. The objective should be the ultimate recall of all troops (except those in a UN police force) to posts within their national boundaries. At this point disengagement must go hand in hand with disarmament. (2) Withdrawal from, or at least critical clarification of, our national commitments to intervene in other nations' wars.

Today the United States appears to have some forty-seven allies to whom we are bound in varying respects and to varying degrees not clearly known to our people, or to most Congressmen, or, one suspects, to the State Department itself. Of these alliances, the one that makes the most sense historically and in relation to the UN is the Organization of American States. That grows out of the Monroe Doctrine and the history of the new world. Because it is regional it fits into a pattern of desirable international organization. There certainly ought to be some type of organization, economic and political, European, American, Asian, African, between the crowd of nations—big, middle-sized, little, and very small—and the inclusive UN. In the better economic organization of today's world there should be great place for a United States of Europe, a closer economic league in the Americas, and other regional federations. To this matter we shall return.

Here it is in order to express grave skepticism of the handouts of second-grade military hardware from Washington to our Latin American neighbors. Some of it has gone to dictators like Trujillo, who make no conceivably good use of it. None of it would be valuable to us in the kind of third world war that might come upon us. Its only use is to give governing cliques something for show, or still worse, something to play with—sometimes against their own people, sometimes against their neighbors. Economic, cooperative aid to Latin America is another matter, which has been too often subordinated to military aid.

Originally, Communist aggression in Europe and Asia made something of a case for NATO* for the defense of Western Europe. It should not now be incontinently abandoned. But it has no sound basis for indefinite continuance as a permanent feature of international organization. It is not a true regional federation since it includes, besides

* I believed, however, that there were then better alternatives. See Chapter VIII and James P. Warburg's *Agenda for Action,* Chapters 1 and 2.

Western Europe, the United States, Greece, and Turkey; it is not a true ideological federation of democracies since it includes fascist Portugal and dubiously democratic Turkey. Western Europe's efforts after economic coopera- tion have bypassed it. It is weakened morally and practi- cally by the British quarrel with Iceland over fishing limits, the three-cornered conflct of Britain, Greece, and Turkey over the situation in Cyprus, and by French absorption in the Algerian conflict, unless De Gaulle can end it. Never- theless, as a military alliance it has a definite meaning for the defense of Western Europe that is well understood, and less likely to get us into trouble than SEATO or the Baghdad Pact.

SEATO adds indefinite commitments for the United States in Asian affairs without adding real strength. Its principal effect has been to disturb or even anger India. And that alone should damn it, because India has a chance by our aid to provide a large-scale demonstration that in Asia and Africa Communism is not the answer to bitter poverty. SEATO is in general an alliance of rulers, not of peoples. The rulers, except in the Philippines, are all dic- tators, not notable for devotion to justice, freedom, or the interests of the masses. The nations over which they rule are not truly free simply because they are non-Communist. It isn't the business of the United States to impose better governments, but our alliance with dictators does not commend itself to our credit as leaders in a truly free world.

Our relation to the Baghdad Pact is worst of all. It was and is a British creation originally intended to under-

gird British oil interests in Iran and Iraq. Such under-
writing of it as Mr. Dulles gave it was one of his major mistakes in the Middle East. Yet when revolution took Iraq
out of a pact which the Iraqi almost universally hated, Mr.
Dulles without even consulting the Senate Foreign Relations Committee, rushed to London to make our commitment to a pact to which we do not formally belong even
stronger. Speaking for a country whose constitution says
that only Congress can declare war, a Secretary of State
encourages British, Turks, and Iranians to think that the
United States will blindly fight any Middle Eastern war
into which they stumble. The danger is greater because we
can trust Turkish courage better than the judgment of
its ruling group. And in Iran the reactionaries, despite the
good intentions of the king and some measures of re-
form, are inviting revolution which we shall be told is all
the fault of indirect, if not direct, aggression from Moscow.

Besides paper alliances, we have great numbers of
very substantial military bases or installations around the
world, 275 of them ringing the Soviet Union. Unquestionably, as a whole they are of military advantage so long as
our policy is based on peace by threat of massive retaliation. The dangers of that policy and the power it necessarily gives to anonymous generals and colonels to plunge
us in war we have already discussed. There is more to be
said about these bases in respect to their bearing on local
and world opinion of us. It is, I think, mostly true that our
government and people sincerely regard these far-flung
forces as defensive and actually as preservers of security
and peace. But in a suspicious world, mindful that his-

torically aggressors have always professed zeal for peace, we cannot expect those bases to be looked upon uncritically, least of all by the Soviet people.

Certain of our bases are not regarded happily by the people of the areas in which they are located. Three of those areas already have manifested a resentment against our bases which makes them a possible source of danger rather than strength to the United States. Militarily weak peoples have proved, as in Indochina, Algeria, and Cyprus, that they can become expert in sabotage. The elaborate installations necessary in modern air bases make them peculiarly vulnerable to sabotage, which can also strike at their various supply lines.

I became conscious of that truth on a brief visit to Rabat, capital of Morocco, in 1953. Outside the capital city was the headquarters for our air bases. An unfriendly government or a hostile people could make these bases untenable, or, if tenable at all, on terms of ill will and struggle against sabotage which would completely offset their military value. Every American observer with whom I have talked or whose opinions I have read believes that we cannot hold these bases, whose construction costs were outrageously high, for five more years without serious trouble. The Eisenhower administration itself is negotiating for only a limited lease. In August 1958, native feeling prevented the unloading of United States munitions ships with cargoes for American bases in Morocco. Our press and radio commentators generally attributed this to resentment at the landing of marines in Lebanon and to Nasser's propaganda. Probably that was the case, but as far back as 1953, before Nasser openly had taken over power in Egypt, there was plenty of smoldering resentment of a Moroccan nationalist sort, intensified by our alliance with the French. One event or another may light the match; the powder is already lying around.

A similar situation is developing in Spain. So important did bases in Spain seem to our military that dictator Franco, put in power by Hitler and Mussolini, has long since been included with the rulers of the free nations whom our government delights to honor. The Pentagon actually gave a medal to General Muñoz Grandes, former Minister of the Army and commander of the Spanish Blue Division who fought for Hitler in Russia. Discontent in Spain is steadily growing, especially among the students and workers. Of course, it is exploited by Communists. Franco is an asset to Communism the world around. But by no means is this anti-Franco feeling a Communist creation. Let me quote a translation of part of a leaflet, a copy of which reached America:

"We work 10 or 12 hours a day just to stay alive, while the thieves and shameless ones live the lives of princes in the world which Franco has created for them. Take a look at our divided Spain, full of Gibraltars [airbases]; take a look at the Americans who inhabit them, how they ostentatiously enjoy something which does not belong to them, how they take our women and then vilely laugh as they relate their 'heroic' adventures."

A third area of potential trouble because of our bases is Okinawa. Recent concessions by the Americans seem to have improved relations. There are some economic advantages to Okinawans because of American spending at the bases. But visitors from Japan tell me that Okinawan feeling still runs against us. The fear once expressed by an anonymous American naval officer that Okinawa could become an American Cyprus still has great validity.

The strategic value of these bases, assuming that they are free from sabotage and that no incident or accident in them precipitates war, is presumably still high. It will become steadily less with the perfection of missiles, including those which can be launched from nuclear-powered submarines. On the other hand, opposition in most countries to the presence of foreign troops (American) on their soil is bound to grow and to be exploited by others as well as by Communists. Hence, even the Pentagon may come to accept considerable disengagement through reduction of the number of bases.

But the disengagement we seek cannot be the mere result of changes in military requirements. It requires plan. It will be most valuable as it goes hand in hand with efforts after universal, controlled disarmament. Communist initiative now embarrasses the United States in Korea; it threatens worse in Germany. The Chinese or Russians say, "We have withdrawn our troops; you do likewise." Such American withdrawals as isolated acts in Korea or Berlin would make bad matters worse. Our failure has been too often to seem on the defensive; we have rarely taken the initiative by proposing workable programs for the Far East, the Middle East, or Middle Europe. Such possible programs require examination.

VII.

Disengagement: The Far East

THE REALLY VITAL areas of our uncertain commitments, those from which major war may come by deliberate intention or by the sudden explosion of a small war into a general conflagration, are three: The Far East (China and Taiwan [Formosa]); the Middle East; and Middle Europe. In all of them, the Middle and Far East and Berlin in Middle Europe, we have been passing through various stages of still unresolved crisis. It is hard to award precedence in immediate danger, but the folly of our commitments is greatest in the Far East where, as Chiang's prisoners, we may yet be involved in a war of great magnitude, possibly growing into a World War III, begun in senseless defense of some rocky islands within cannon shot of the Chinese mainland.

A temporary escape from this war will not of itself deliver us from the dangers of our blind insistence that the warlord, Chiang, ingloriously driven to Taiwan behind the protection of our Seventh Fleet, is entitled to represent vast China in the United Nations.

How we got into our present incredible position, supported—except under our pressure—by none of our major allies, is something of a mystery. It was, indeed, a shock that Chiang, whom we had backed so extensively and uncritically, was so easily and ingloriously driven out of China, not by the Russians, but by Chinese Communists. Any increase in Communist power was, of course, deplorable. Further, the Chinese role in the attack on Korea was outrageous. But that did not justify the Truman and Eisenhower administrations in their refusal to face certain hard facts both before and after the Korean war. Here are the facts our wishful thinkers ignored:

(1) Chiang's government of China, while less ruthlessly cruel than the Communists', has been described by the informed historian, Professor John King Fairbank of Harvard, in terms of ideological sterility, suppression of criticism, fiscal mismanagement and military incompetence. It had no real popular support among many intelligent anti-Communists. This was brought home to me in 1952 when I was briefly in Hong Kong.

I was invited to a very private dinner with a group of earnest Chinese, anti-Communists, calling themselves, as I remember it, the Freedom Front. In the face of the Communist record of cruelty and denial of freedom and the Communist aggression in Korea, I was very sympathetic with them. But I was surprised at the detailed indictment they all gave me of Chiang, or, more accurately, of his ministers and agents, especially the Soong family, to which Madame Chiang belonged. One of the older men said: "The difference between Chiang's government and the Communist is this: All Chiang's officials were bad and corrupt. Mao's government is bad and corrupt in its heart." A younger man, the apparent leader who had been educated in America, assured me that the initiative for China's freedom must come from within, that it must be supported by American men and arms to which Chiang's forces could only be auxiliary, and that in victory Chiang could never rule China.

(2) Cruelly totalitarian as Mao's government has been and is, according to the almost unanimous testimony of foreign observers—the State Department won't allow us Americans to go to see for ourselves—it has effectively united vast China as that ancient country has not been united for generations; it has made great progress in sanitation, education, industrialization, and military strength. One year has followed another without evidence that the undoubted discontent is strong enough to challenge seriously Mao's grim but dedicated Communist builders of a new China. Not even the recent absorption of peasants into communes totally controlling their lives seems to have aroused a serious threat of rebellion.

(3) There was a case for delaying the UN's recognition of Mao's government to see if it was effectively established. There was an overwhelming case for excluding it from the UN while it supported the Korean war against the UN. There never was any case for allowing Chiang indefinitely to represent not Taiwan but the coun-

try from which he had been expelled. Chiang's position even in Taiwan is not that of a true democratic president. The Taiwanese were not asked if they wanted him and his refugee army. Before his expulsion from the mainland, Chiang's officials celebrated our return of Taiwan to Chiang's China by massacring some 5,000 Taiwanese. Today the government is described as fairly good with a high level of living by Asian standards, thanks to our prodding, our technical advice, and the $2,500,000,000 of military and economic aid that we have poured in. But there is little democracy. As recently as August 31, 1958, after the Communist bombardment of Quemoy had begun, Tillman Durdin in the New York *Times* reported in some detail the grievances of the Taiwanese against Chiang and his army. Not many months ago in the island which we saved from the Communists, Americans were the objects of serious Taiwanese rioting. It has even been suggested that Chiang's army might not prove completely loyal against Communist interpenetration and Communist attack. It is, however, very well-trained (by Americans) and very well-armed (by Americans), even to the possession of Sidewinder missiles for the airforce. It seems to have fought loyally and efficiently in Quemoy.

(4) The UN is enormously weakened by the exclusion from it of the effective government of the world's largest nation, a nation which is rapidly growing in power. To be effective the UN must be inclusive. Despite certain moral and not wholly hypocritical clauses in its charter, the UN was not formed as a League of the Good. (Had it been, who should stand?) It properly included from

the beginning the Soviet Union as a major power although Stalin and his party were, if anything, guilty of more abominable crimes against humanity on the road to power and in power than the Chinese Communists. China's exclusion from the UN means that Peiping must depend on Russian veto of any action it may regard as hurtful, even although China very clearly is no mere satellite of the Soviet Union. Both nations, Russian and Chinese, are under pressure from outside to act together, whatever natural differences of interest might tend on certain issues to divide them. A common Communist faith would not of itself have that effect. Witness the history of divisions among Communists in Russia, and what is more pertinent, Tito's revolt against Russian domination. There is some evidence that Khrushchev, who left Mao out of his Middle Eastern plans, was brought into line by Mao and constrained to support his attack on Quemoy.

Already the result of this situation is to doom the Security Council of the UN, intended as a major instrument of peace, to near impotence. The Soviet Union can protect its own interest and China's by the veto and nothing more. The West, so far, is sufficiently united under American leadership and pressure to dominate the Council and the other instrumentalities of the UN. (How that worked in the Trusteeship Council on the question of banning nuclear tests in the Marshall Islands, I have told in a previous chapter.)

The disadvantages to us may be illustrated by supposing that, through bypassing the Security Council, we could get a substantial agreement on first steps in disarmament in the Assembly. Russia could nominally accept the agreement and then cooperate with China, outside the UN, to build up strength untouched by agreement. Or if Moscow for its own interest wanted agreement on a beginning of disarmament, its desire could be frustrated by the threat to us of a vindictive China steadily growing in industrial power, but excluded from the UN. In a world where the alternative to war must be effective negotiation of agreements in and under the UN, we offer China no part in the alternative. Only war is left to her.

In the face of these facts, the logical consequences of which have been recognized by most of our principal allies, the United States has insisted that its puppet, Chiang, must represent China. Year after year by a diminishing margin it has been able to make the Assembly vote to postpone consideration of the situation. This year (1958) in an obviously reluctant Assembly, it once more won postponement by a vote of 44 to 28 with 9 abstentions— the smallest margin yet, even though at the time the vote was taken, Red China was technically an aggressor by its bombardment of Quemoy. Some observers think the vote would have been very different if it could have been secret. But our power, our good deeds—we have some to our credit—and our pressure on our friends carried us through, perhaps for the last or next to the last time. Canada, the New York *Times* informed us, intended to announce that this would be her last vote for postponement and was only dissuaded by enormous pressure, including a threat that such an announcement might jeopardize our alliance.

Of course, this sort of thing can't go on indefinitely, even if we escape war over Quemoy. Sooner or later the effective government of China will be admitted despite our disapproval, and our obstinacy will have brought us a defeat more damaging to our face throughout the world than if even now we should deal on our own motion with the situation, and propose the seating of Mao on condition that the Korean truce be turned into peace and that China give assurances of nonaggression against her neighbors, including Taiwan, which, under UN protection, should be given a later opportunity in an atmosphere of peace to decide its own fate by plebiscite.

But instead of turning to anything so reasonable, the Administration as I write is not yet free from its crowning and most dangerous folly: its insistence that we should risk war to assure that Quemoy and Matsu, small islands within gunshot of the mainland and commanding the harbors of Amoy and Fuchow, should remain in Chiang's hands. After Congress, by Joint Resolution in 1955, approved Eisenhower's pledge to protect Taiwan, giving him discretionary power to include Quemoy and Matsu, Chiang deliberately weakened his forces on Taiwan by putting thousands of men on Quemoy, thereby giving him a right to claim our protection because their loss would weaken him. These islands are only in Chiang's hands because our Seventh Fleet intervened before the Communists could complete their mopping-up operation. No government on the mainland could be expected to leave them forever in hostile hands any more than our Revolutionary forefathers would have been prepared to leave Block

Island in British hands on the plea that it was necessary
to British protection of Newfoundland.

The off-shore islands are only valuable to Chiang if
he should become strong enough to use them to invade
the mainland or as bait to drag us into an aggressive war
against Red China by reason of a blank commitment to
support him against the Communists, whatever he may do.
Indeed, on September 30 the New York *Times* carried a
letter from David Nelson Rowe of Yale, recently returned
from conducting "academic research" on Taiwan, in which
he categorically declared that "Chinese Nationalist forces
are in Quemoy and Matsu today only because American
military advisers some years ago urged President Chiang
Kai-shek, against his expressed interest, to keep them
there." Unfortunately for Professor Rowe, on the very day
that his letter was published (September 30), Secretary
Dulles, in what was universally regarded as a marked re-
versal or modification of his policy, told his news conference a very different story.

Before that date the volume of protest here and
abroad had been growing. An amazingly apathetic public
gradually awoke to the meaning of our apparent slavery
to Chiang's decisions. Leaders like Adlai Stevenson be-
latedly got around to saying that the defense of Taiwan
did not mean the defense of Quemoy and Matsu. In this
atmosphere Mr. Dulles told his press conference "The
United States did not feel that it was sound to make the
major commitments of force to those areas [Quemoy and
Matsu] that the Chinese Government wished to make. In
view, however, of the very strong views of the Republic

of China (Chiang) we were acquiescent in that." He
added that "We do not have any legal commitments to
defend the offshore islands." Moreover, he declared that
in the event of a cease-fire in the area "which seemed to
be reasonably dependable, I think it would be foolish to
keep these large forces on the islands. We thought it
rather foolish to put them there and, as I say, if there were
a cease-fire it would be our judgment, military judgment
even, that it would not be wise or prudent to keep them
there."

These words, later echoed by the President, were very
different from anything the Administration had previously
said publicly or allowed the world to think that its spokesman, Ambassador Beam, was authorized to say in his
negotiations with Mao's representative at Warsaw. They
shocked Chiang, who insisted that he would never withdraw any of his troops.

About this time Mao's government, perhaps finding
the offshore islands a harder nut to crack than it had expected, announced a two weeks' cessation of their bombardment and began publicly to plead with the Taiwanese
and even Chiang himself to transfer their loyalty to the
Communist State.

The hard-working Mr. Dulles flew to Taiwan and ex-
tracted, for the first time, from Chiang a statement that
he had no intention of trying to invade the mainland unless to help a revolution from within. This kind of declaration at this juncture was widely interpreted as a step on
the Administration's part to acceptance of the two-Chinas
policy with a withdrawal of troops from the offshore

islands, provided that the Communists would definitely cease fire.

On the contrary, Mao's government renewed its bombardment which, as I write, is on a curious and inhumane every-other-day basis. It insists that its objective is Taiwan itself and the end of American imperialism in the West Pacific. It does not, however, show any present intention of all-out invasion even of Quemoy, to say nothing of Taiwan.

These are not satisfactory conditions for negotiating peace in the Formosa Straits, but neither do they seem to present the immediate threat of war on the scale of the Korean conflict or the world war into which that conflict might grow. (Khrushchev has said that the Soviet Union would fight alongside China only if the mainland should be invaded with American support.) The UN is concerned for peace.

We have, then, no settlement of crisis in the Far East, but a lessening of tension. Mao's government may be completely obdurate and demand immediately all or nothing. But this we can not know until our government has tried to advance a rational program of constructive disengagement in the Far East. This, I suggest, requires (1) evacuation of Quemoy and Matsu; (2) seating of the effective government of China in the UN and its recognition by the United States on condition that the Korean truce be turned into peace; and (3) an agreement that the government of Taiwan continue unmolested under UN protection until such time as in an atmosphere of peace the islanders for the first time can decide their own fate by plebiscite. It requires also abandonment of Mr. Dulles' contention that diplomatic recognition can properly be used as a tool in the service of national interest. That it cannot be in any sound international order.

VIII.

Disengagement: The Middle East

A FAVORITE cliché refers to the Middle East as a witches' cauldron of troubles. The cliché errs if it is meant to imply that the ingredients in the brew are more or less than human. On the contrary they are human, all too human desires, hates, and prejudices. We are dealing with peoples moving out of a quasi-feudalistic society, cursed with landlordism, blessed—or cursed?—with oil which other people covet, animated by nationalism which mostly takes the form of a pan-Arabism, deeply offended by the intrusion of a lusty young Israel.

These generalizations apply most closely to the Arab Middle East, but the geographic area usually is held to include also Turkey, Iran, and Pakistan. Aside from geography, the unifying principle—if any—of this larger area is religion and a somewhat similar economy and culture. These peoples are in overwhelming majority followers of the Prophet Mohammed. But Islam, like Christianity, is divided into sects; Turks, Iranians, and Pakistani do not speak Arabic, and their loves and hates are not the same as those of the Arab peoples whom the Turks ruled until their defeat in World War I.

It is primarily American involvement in the Arab areas of the Middle East which requires disengagement. Our involvement arises out of concern for Arabian oil, and our sense of responsibility for Israel. On both counts we are peculiarly concerned lest the area fall prey to "Nasserism"—the popular description of pan-Arabism, which in turn, most Americans fear, will be the dupe, or the ally, of Soviet imperialism.

We have taken over from the British and French and, if possible, have magnified the Western desire to exclude Russia from her immediate neighbor, the Middle East, Arabic and non-Arabic. Of that there is no longer any possibility. The task is as impossible as it would be for the USSR to cut us off from Central America. A serious attempt would be an excellent road to war. The best we can hope from the Arab world is an honest and constructive military neutrality. The attempt to get more will be as ill-fated as was the inclusion of the Iraq of the great land-owners in the Baghdad Pact. That was an important reason for the revolution which took over the whole country in twenty-four hours. The Pact was almost universally regarded and resented in the Arab world as an attempt "to divide Arab brothers" and to force a dangerous participation on the American side in the cold war. (I speak with some confidence as the result of my experiences during

November and December, 1957, in the Middle East, where
I and my companion, the Middle-East specialist Dr. Don
Peretz, were fortunate enough to have many contacts.)

Shortly before World War I, nationalism began to stir
the Arab peoples, who for four centuries had been under
the rule of the Turks, fellow believers but not friends and
comrades. This feeling increased during the war in which
Arab help was a boon to the Allies. The Arabs, however,
despite promises, were not rewarded with national freedom except in the most backward area, the Arabian peninsula. Britain had made too many conflicting promises to
Arabs, French, and Zionists. So after a period of confusion,
five nascent states emerged out of what had been Turkish
territory, undivided by clear-cut boundaries into potentially separate nations. These were Syria and Lebanon
under French mandate; Iraq, Jordan, and Palestine under
British mandate. Egypt, whose people, despite their use
of the Arabic language, did not then regard themselves so
much Arabs as Egyptians, remained under British over-
lordship principally because of British interest in the Suez
Canal.

The Balfour Declaration of 1917 had promised the
Jews a homeland in Palestine. In that historic land, sacred
to three religions, there was indeed room under modern
development for a much larger population. But the land
was by no means empty. It was the dwelling-place of
Arabs, mostly Moslem, whose ancestors had lived there
continuously for centuries. Zionist ardor demanded that
a homeland be turned into a state; Hitler's enormous
cruelty gave desperate political urgency to the Jewish de-

sire to re-establish a nation of their own in the ancient territories of Israel. This desire clashed with Arab nationalism, and the efforts of Dr. Judah Magnes, chancellor of the Hebrew University, and others, to reconcile Arab and Jewish nationalisms in a bi-national state were rejected by both sides.

Immediately after World War II the situation had developed thus: Palestine, still under British Mandate, was torn by quarrels between Arabs and the new Israeli people who had begun building a remarkable state long before the British mandate was ended. All the Arab states were now independent, but Britain still controlled the Suez Canal Zone. Oil, which was of increasingly urgent importance to Western Europe, was the chief treasure of otherwise barren areas in the Arabian Peninsula and also of Iraq. The British held concessions in Iraq and the tiny Arabian sheikdoms of Bahrein and Kuwait, immensely rich in oil. Aramco, primarily an American concern, operated in King Ibn Saud's territory—by far the largest part of the peninsula. To keep control of oil in the hands of the West became a primary concern of diplomacy.

As time went on, a "freedom-loving nation" in the Middle East became identified as such if its ruling clique opposed Communism and cooperated with the West. Nothing mattered but oil, and for that the West was willing, perforce, to pay the existing rulers very well.

Unfortunately the ruling clique around the king in Iraq were landlords; King Ibn Saud and later his son were medieval Arab autocrats who still kept chattel slaves. A middle class, literate, desirous of industrial progress and some degree of social and political reforms, was emerging. Nationalism was increasingly pan-Arabic, not particularist: Iraqi, Syrian, Jordanian.

How this situation might have developed with special reference to friendship for the West, rather than the Soviet Union, had there been no Israel, is anybody's guess. There was resentment against the former colonial powers, British and French, especially the British in Egypt where British troops controlled the canal zone. The United States had played no imperial role and Americans, notably at the famous University of Beirut, had established or helped to establish important educational centers.

But there was Israel. British efforts to limit Jewish immigration into Palestine broke down. Neither the United States nor any other nation opened wide its doors to refugees from European oppressors. It was more satisfactory to give sympathy and money to the Zionists. Where should the Jews go but to Palestine? British restrictions were generally disapproved of in America; the struggles between well-organized Jewish communities and the disorganized Arabs became more intense.

Post-war Britain, struggling with her own problems and in weariness, abandoned her Palestinian mandate in 1947, throwing the whole tangled problem into the lap of the infant United Nations. That organization finally accepted a partition plan, assigning to Israel those areas in which Jews were by any margin, however slight, the more numerous, and it internationalized Jerusalem. A map of Palestine thus divided was fantastic; Jewish areas only met at what the Israeli dubbed "kissing points." But the UN on

paper compensated for that by a pious hope of economic
unity for the area.

The Jews reluctantly accepted the UN proposal; the
Arabs rejected it, and the badly organized Arab states
with ill-trained armies made common war on the Jews.
The disproportion of Jewish strength to Arab was very
great, but the Jewish David won a notable victory over
a lumbering, ill-coordinated, and ill-armed Arab Goliath.
When in 1948 an armistice was brought about by the
United Nations representative, Ralph Bunche, the Jews
held considerably more territory than had been assigned
them by the armistice. Out of the whole territory there had
been a wholesale flight of Arabs, leaving land and houses
to land-hungry Jewish immigrants. The armistice lines
were understood to be based on the military situation and
subject to adjustment in the peace settlement which ten
years later seems far more remote than it then seemed to
Mr. Bunche. Behind the armistice lines Israel was
promptly recognized by President Truman and almost as
promptly by Stalin.

The new state within these limits was more viable
than in the UN partition but there was no hope of economic cooperation in a situation progressively embittered
by the flight of the refugees and the fact that the Arabs
who had not fled were in many respects, largely for security
reasons, treated like second-class citizens. The Arab states,
arguing that legally a state of war still existed, imposed an
economic blockade on Israel. Every effort was made on
both sides to keep their respective areas hermetically
closed to their neighbors. The armistice boundaries not

only divided Jerusalem with a rigor unknown in divided Berlin but separated many villages from their farmlands. The situation invited the sniping and raids and counter-raids which have occurred.

The parts of Palestine—the whole of it about the size of Vermont—not occupied by the Israeli were annexed by King Abdullah of Jordan, except for the Gaza Strip occupied by Egypt and filled with refugees. Sparsely populated Jordan, artificially divided by Britain from Iraq and Syria, had got along as a fairly homogeneous Bedouin country aided by a British subsidy. It was weakened, not strengthened, by the addition of regions whose people considered themselves of higher culture but who brought no great economic assets. It was further weakened by the great flood of refugees still quartered in its territories.

Of those refugees and their children there are now about 1,000,000, mostly housed in refugee camps under the care of the UN in the various Arab countries and fed at a per capita of about 7¢ a day. These human beings have been treated as pawns in a political struggle for ten years. The Arab states have blocked their resettlement and done little or nothing to help them get even temporary work. Only Jordan has made them citizens. The Israeli have paid them not one cent for their land and buildings which they have occupied for more than ten years. These Arabs nominally still own the larger part of privately owned arable lands in Israel. All Israeli offers of repatriation have had strings tied to them and only about 35,000 have been readmitted.

It is amazing that the UN camps are as orderly and

well run as they are, but they are badly supported, so badly
that the efforts of Henry Labouisse, until recently director
of the UN Relief and Works Agency for Palestine Refugees
in the Near East, to provide trade schools were checked by
lack of funds. Little more can be done than to provide ele-
mentary education for children. The older people live
on dreams of return. They tell their little children that
they belong to the towns and villages of their fathers. I
asked some little girls playing in a camp, through an inter-
preter, where they were born. They had all been born in
camps but all answered cheerfully by naming their family
villages.

In one of the small handful of better camps, in fact a
kind of model village near Damascus supported in part
by Syrian funds, a vigorous but elderly Arab received two
of us American visitors in the attractive little garden or
patio of his small but tidy home. His sons, like many others
from that village but unlike most refugees, had jobs to
which they went by bus to Damascus. After some general
conversation we asked him if he and his family would not
like to stay in so pleasant a place. The reply in a torrent of
Arab eloquence was that he only lived to return home. On
our visit to Musa Bey Alami's remarkable school for
orphan boys near Jericho, we had a charming young Arab
as our guide. One of us inquired if the school was not also
a resettlement colony. "Don't use that bad word," said our
guide. "We only want to go home."

The Israeli say that the Arabs did not have to fly
before or during the Arab war; that they went exhorted by
their misleaders, who promised a return in triumph; that

Israel would like to settle the problem of these refugees along with other problems as part of a general peace settlement; that Israel probably could and would take back some refugees but that neither the Israeli nor the Arabs would be happy if all or most of the latter were repatriated into a Jewish state needing room for Jewish immigrants, a state very different from the communities which the Arabs had left.

The Arabs say that the refugees fled in terror because of threats to them or the example of Israeli atrocities like the massacre during the war in the Arab village of Dyer Yassim. In my presence, my traveling companion, Dr. Don Peretz, author of the authoritative and objective book, *Israel and the Palestine Arabs,* asked every individual in a group of about a dozen men, all refugees, why he and his family had fled. Each one alleged some threat or actual coercive pressure. The picture seemed to me one of panic flight of a sort quite usual in the tradition of the wars of oriental lands. Justice, the Arabs unanimously declared, required that the United States prove its friendship by insisting, in and out of the UN, upon their return.

This demand of the refugees is echoed or rather encouraged by the governments of the Arab states, in Lebanon, and in Iraq before the revolution, as much as in Syria or Egypt. Indeed, except for the young King Hussein of Jordan, Nasser in November 1957 was about the least bitter and insistent on this subject of all the prominent Arab leaders to whom I talked. Perhaps the reason was lack of time, since most of our conversation dealt with conditions in Egypt. At any rate, he gave us no such anti-

Israeli lecture as did Dr. Jamali of Baghdad, high in the old Iraqi government and an avowed friend of the West.

When I was briefly in Cairo in the summer of 1953 before the Israeli and Anglo-French attack on Egypt in 1956, Egypt's Foreign Secretary Fawzi had told me that his country did not want to drive the Israeli into the sea; Egyptians only wanted the refugees resettled somewhere, but not in overpopulated Egypt. Beyond that, they insisted that Israel should not be a "barricade" between them and their Arab brothers. According to a story in the New York *Times* (August 31, 1958), Mr. Fawzi in behalf of the United Arab Republic proposed to the revived Arab League that it ask the big powers to join the Arab states and Israel in a declaration pledging nonaggression and nonintervention in the area. The matter was dropped, but the conciliating resolution for which Fawzi was largely responsible was pushed through the UN Assembly. Fawzi's stand, if it was as reported, is the best news to come out of the Middle East recently, but subsequent statements from Cairo awoke suspicions of the report.

The general Arab belief is that in our American dealings with the Middle East, our actions are controlled by the strong American Zionists. Toward the end of 1957 I called on the "red millionaire" Kahleb el Azam, Defense Minister of Syria, who had negotiated an advantageous loan from the Soviet Union. His Excellency was not a Communist, but he was anti-American and pro-Soviet. I took occasion to remind him that back in 1946, Jan Masaryk of Czechoslovakia had been as optimistic as he was about his ability to manage the Russians, but that in the end Masaryk was either thrown out of a window to his death by Communists or driven by despair to suicide. El Azam made light of it as certainly suicide, and said, "Didn't your Forrestal do the same—driven in his case by Zionists?" (Something of the caliber of the Minister of Defense was shown by the fact that while he was putting sandbags in the streets of Damascus in the trumped-up Turkish war scare of the summer of 1957—some of the bags were still in front of his palatial house at the time of my call—he rented its ground floor to the Turkish Embassy. On the consummation of Syrian-Egyptian unity he fled Damascus to sanctuary, I am told, in "the American quarter of Beirut.")

One of the advantages that Moscow has in the Arab world is that although Stalin raced Truman to recognize Israel and although Russia has spent not one cent to keep the Arab refugees alive, she is not regarded, as we are, as committed to Israel.

But before we examine our various commitments in the Middle East it is necessary to look briefly at the phenomenon known as Nasserism and our dealing with it. Nasserism is supposed to be a type of personal imperialism into which pan-Arabism has degenerated, a threat to the independence of Arab nations from the Persian Gulf to the Strait of Gibraltar. Nasser in our press and over the radio is frequently compared to Hitler, Stalin, or, at best, Mussolini. For all his pretensions to power he is assumed to be the ally or dupe of Moscow and therefore of great concern to us in the cold war. I do not write as an authority on Gamal Abdel Nasser on the basis of a study of the record plus an hour and a half talk with him, but I dare to say that the too-easy comparison of him with Hitler is certainly incorrect, as none other than Ben-Gurion admitted in reply to a question in a broadcast interview.

Nasser was a young Egyptian army officer, humiliated and disgusted by the corruption and inefficiency of his government as it was revealed to him in the Israeli war. With like-minded officers he brought about a virtually bloodless revolution and the expulsion of King Farouk. He told me that the group did not want to take power but only to clean house. (He still lives with his family in comparative simplicity.) The young men were forced to take power, he said, and being inexperienced, made many mistakes. His first interest was Egypt and in November 1957 he (and, later, his ambassador in Damascus, General Riad) seemed far more lukewarm on unity with Syria than the enthusiastic Syrians. One of Nasser's ministers told us that he thought Iraq and Syria could take two or three million Egyptian farmers in the lands they were irrigating and thus relieve, temporarily, Egyptian overpopulation. Nasser said that he doubted it; Egyptians, like himself, were home-lovers. "When I come back from traveling and my plane is over the Nile, I say: 'Ah, this is home.'" Undoubtedly today he is a pan-Arabist with a sense of call to leadership. He believes, he says, in democratic socialism but is opposed to political parties. But his Parliament, elected in the summer of 1957 after hot electoral campaigns between individual candidates, all of whose loyalty was approved, was far from a rubber-stamp affair at the time of my visit.

According to Nasser's own book, he shares a pan-Arab dream of expansion and, what is worse, his radio and press are often unscrupulous in inciting the people of neighboring countries to rebellion and to assassination of rulers. (Nasser complained to us that some "Baghdad Pact" radio or radios "in Cyprus" did as much against him. Assassination has been an all-too-common method of political action in all the Middle East.) He will take help where he can get it, but what he wants is neutrality in the cold war. Tito is his great friend, not Khrushchev.

By and large I think that, although he has become not only the symbol but the leader of pan-Arabism, insofar as that vague but passionate movement has a leader, he is less pan-Arabism's creator than its creature, exalted in the minds of Arabs by the results of the Suez crisis despite the bad showing of Egyptian arms. If one could have imagined a fair plebiscite in Iraq or Jordan at the time of my visit, Nasser, I am convinced, would have won hands down against the young kings whose unpopularity was less their fault than the fault of the governing cliques who were regarded not only as corrupt but as enemies of pan-Arabism, too closely tied in with the West.

I heard an American whose experience gave him some right to be considered an expert on the Middle East answer in three words a lady who asked him, "Could anyone be worse than Nasser?" He said: "Yes, his successor." The British and French could have made no greater error than to think that their invasion could rather easily result in the secure establishment of a docile or friendly regime in Egypt.

Despite President Eisenhower's firm and wise support of the UN in condemnation of the Suez invasion, Washington's handling of the Middle East in general and Nasser in particular has been marked by blunders, the basic error being its apparent assumption that we could make the Arab states virtually our allies in the cold war. Perhaps that hope, added to regard for human values, made Mr. Dulles promise great help to Nasser in building the Aswan Dam, which might give more water to irrigate desperately needed new acreage for overpopulated Egypt. Even in Egypt I met men with reservations about the dam and our offer, but it was definitely made. And then, because Nasser had bought arms where he could get them, namely from Czechoslovakia, Dulles withdrew his offer in a manner most offensive to an Oriental's pride. Thereupon Nasser suddenly nationalized the Suez Canal in order, allegedly, to increase Egyptian revenue. British forces, to British regret, had been for sometime withdrawn from the area; Nasser's action was supported in international law; he rapidly proved able to operate the canal efficiently and he promised proper compensation to the stockholders of the old company, a promise later fulfilled. The West finally submitted with ill grace but kept its fears that its oil supplies might be cut off or made difficult of access. France was also angered by Egyptian moral support of, and clandestine aid to, the Algerian rebels.

Israel meanwhile was angered by especially persistent air raids from Egypt, the answer apparently to an earlier Israeli raid on the Gaza Strip. Ben-Gurion determined on a major attack on Egypt across the Sinai Peninsula. With or without preliminary secret agreement, France and Britain then determined on a joint attack which took place during October and November 1956. The Israeli military attack was relatively better and more successfully managed than the Anglo-French. Egyptian military resistance was not impressive. But the United Nations, backed by the moral force of the United States and by a Soviet threat to intervene with volunteers, saved Egypt and Nasser, and eventually brought about a return to the status quo with the addition of the first UN police force to patrol the border of the Gaza Strip. The net result built up Nasser's fame in the Arab world and imperiled the close alliance of the Western Powers.

It is now the fashion in many quarters to think and say that President Eisenhower should have let the British and French finish their job. Under the circumstances, that would have been a blow to the UN from which it would with difficulty have recovered. There was an excellent chance that Russian "volunteers" would have intervened with consequent risk of world war. In any event, the Anglo-French success would have turned the Arab world into a vast Algeria of sabotage and terror against the West in general and its oil interests in particular. Modern history proves that nations incapable of effective war in the nuclear age can become adept at sabotage and guerrilla tactics against the stronger powers who must guard complex facilities, railway lines, etc.

For a time after Suez, American prestige was high in the Arab world. But not for long. Perhaps in order to appease the anger of our allies, Mr. Dulles in word and deed left little undone to harass Nasser. Repeatedly it was thrown up to Dr. Peretz and myself in the Middle East that the United States had withdrawn from Egypt that admirable philanthropic agency, CARE, and blocked Egyptian funds in American banks (nominally to protect the canal's stockholders) so that Nasser could not use them to buy wheat or Salk vaccine. By November 1957 a Copt, not one of Nasser's eulogists, a professor in the great Cairo University, friendly to the West, told us with regret that in the student body America had become more unpopular than Britain. The students said, "We at least know where the British stand."

The Eisenhower Doctrine, proclaiming an American commitment to protect the nations against external aggression, was not well-received by its potential beneficiaries, and American support of the Baghdad Pact was deeply resented. In February 1957 the Soviet government had proposed a kind of neutralization of the Middle East in the following terms:

"1. The preservation of peace in the Near and Middle East by settling outstanding questions exclusively by peaceful means and by the method of negotiations;

"2. Non-interference in the internal affairs of Middle Eastern countries, and respect for their sovereignty and independence;

"3. Renunciation of all attempts to involve these countries in military blocs with the participation of the Great Powers;

"4. Liquidation of foreign bases and withdrawal of

foreign troops from the territory of Middle Eastern countries;

"5. Reciprocal refusal to deliver arms to Middle Eastern countries;

"6. Promotion of the Middle Eastern nations' economic development without attaching any political, military or other terms incompatible with the dignity and sovereignty of these countries."

Obviously the State Department could not have accepted this note from Bulganin out of hand (especially since it would apply to our ally, Turkey) but it made a fundamental error in ignoring it rather than trying to make it the basis for constructive discussion. Later, when the launching of the sputnik carried Russian military prestige to a great height, some Arabs held that probably the United States was as inferior to Russia in strength as its attitude toward the Bulganin note proved it to be in desire for peace.

Mr. Dulles did not help matters by his handling of Syrian affairs. In the summer of 1957, greatly perturbed by what he considered an alarmingly pro-Soviet coalition cabinet in Syria and later by the Turkish war scare magnified by Soviet propaganda, he first gave the Arabs—and others—the impression that the United States might extend the Eisenhower Doctrine to apply against internal Communist subversion or resolution—an impression the Administration had to correct in the case of Syria. Then he arranged a flamboyant arms drop to Jordan which a Jordanian told me did little to strengthen that country but which annoyed Syria on one hand and Israel on the other. It was a policy that won us respect neither for firmness nor friendship.

Early in 1958 came the consummation of the union of Syria with Egypt in the United Arab Republic, which later joined autocratically governed little Yemen to it in federation but not organic union. The governing groups in Iraq and Jordan—not the people—in answer to this union joined together Iraq and Jordan, a union which, had it worked, would at least have made Jordan a part of a viable state not in danger of momentary collapse. All those major actions were attended by numerous political maneuvers unimportant to the present discussion.

Rather surprisingly to most of the West, the pot first boiled over in Lebanon, the one Arab state in which Christians have, or think they have, a majority over the Moslems, the state with the highest per capita income, and the state most friendly to the West. It was hard to understand just what the revolt was about. Lebanon exists separately from Syria because when the French set it up, it had a Christian majority. But there has been no census since 1932; the Moslems thought they now had a majority, and that the gentlemen's agreement regarding the distribution of offices among sects should be revised. A third religious group, the Druses, were also discontent. Not only Moslems and Druses but also some Christians believed that the parliamentary elections had been rigged by President Chamoun's government; he was accused of seeking re-election requiring constitutional revision by that same parliament. Along with all this went the charge that the government was dragging Lebanon into the cold war, that it gave only hypocritical lip service to pan-Arabism, that at the least, the government should try to make Lebanon a kind of neutral Switzerland of the Middle East.

It was the assassination of the vehemently pro-Arab editor, Metni, which triggered the revolt. Dr. Peretz and I had called on him when he was recovering from a former assassination attempt by government men. He assured us that he was not anti-American except as Americans opposed pan-Arabism and that he was not Communist.

Indeed there was no evidence of Communism in the revolt. Two of the leaders were rich men, ex-premiers; the one, Saeb Salem, whom I met, was certainly no Communist. A third, Kemal Jumblatt, was at once head of a powerful Druse family, leader of the Progressive Socialists, a student of Indian philosophy, and less than an enthusiastic eulogist of all Nasser's policies. It wasn't Nasser's revolt although his radio indulged in "indirect aggression." There was some interpenetration, probably inevitable given the geography and history of the country—the Druses, for instance, are primarily Druses whether they live in Lebanon or Syria.

President Eisenhower probably would not have acceded to President Chamoun's request for American troops had it not been for the sudden revolution in Iraq. He and the British found themselves too late to save the Iraqi government but presumed that by their troop landings in Lebanon and Jordan the West had shown that it could not be shoved around. Khrushchev condemned the landings, but made no such definite threats as in the Suez affair.

He wanted no war and had reason to be content with his progress in Arab opinion as their great friend asking less of them than did the West.

The American troops, some 20,000 in all, were landed without untoward incident under orders, faithfully observed, not to interfere in Lebanon's civil war which went on smoldering with occasional flare-ups. The diplomatic game was transferred to the UN where, after much backing and filling on the part both of Moscow and Washington, a special meeting of the UN General Assembly was called. Its only concern was with aggression, direct and indirect. President Eisenhower addressed it in a speech more considerate of the ideal of pan-Arabism and the need of constructive economic aid in the Middle East than his Administration's earlier statements would imply. Somewhat surprisingly and very intelligently the old Arab League pulled itself together, and the Arab nations including Lebanon proposed that the Secretary General and UN observers give sanction to a general policy of nonaggression.

Don Peretz, writing from Lebanon to the *Progressive* (November 1958) comments:

"Any hope for 'checking Nasserism' which might have inspired the landing of British and American troops in the Middle East was completely undermined by the ten-nation Arab resolution passed by the UN General Assembly on August 21, which again presented Nasser an opportunity for 'statesmanship.' His 'moderation' and 'cooperation,' plus the aid of UN Secretary-General Dag Hammarskjöld, enabled the U. S. and Great Britain to withdraw discreetly.

Since it showed that the Arab states were basically united when it came to foreign intervention, the resolution was a great victory for the nationalism which Secretary Dulles has been trying to 'contain.' "

The ten Arab nations did not stay united except in opposition to outside intervention. The new Iraqi government is having its troubles with too extreme pro-Nasserites. But when, according to promise, President Eisenhower withdrew the American forces from Lebanon at the end of October, it left a Lebanon which had finally ended what had become a disgraceful war between Christians and Moslems (Dr. Peretz believes that the presence of American troops had tended to prolong rather than shorten that war). In any case, we left a country with a government far more neutralist and pan-Arabist than when our troops landed. British withdrawal from Jordan leaves that artificial kingdom as insecure as it was before its short-lived union with Iraq. In Iraq itself there is increasing evidence that opposition to Nasser is largely pro-Communist, inspired and encouraged by the Kremlin, which has even less use for an effective pan-Arab federation than Mr. Dulles.

One or two influential Beirut papers contrasted the American troop withdrawal with Russian actions in Hungary in terms very favorable to the United States. But, by a sobering coincidence, for a second time, Western actions in the Middle East blessed Communism by diverting attention from Hungary; the first, the Suez crisis at the time of the Russian invasion of Hungary; the second, the American troop landing soon after the report of the outrageous execution of former-Premier Nagy and other Hungarian patriots. The unfortunate timing of events was illustrated by its effect on an activity with which I have been closely involved. Before the Lebanese crisis, the Institute of International Labor Research, which has been interested in popular education in what Communism really means to the people under it, sent out forty-four cables to leaders in labor and civic circles in Latin American, Asian, and African countries asking them to arouse popular support for a special session of the UN Assembly to consider the Hungarian situation in the light of continuing executions of a sort condemned by the report of the UN Committee on the Hungarian revolt. The Institute received 161 very favorable replies, many from Latin American countries where Communist parties seem to be making headway and the moral campaign against Communism is of primary importance. Secretary General Hammarskjöld, Sir Leslie Munor, president of the General Assembly, and our Ambassador Henry Cabot Lodge were informed of these replies. All this went for naught because it was suddenly overshadowed by the American landing in Lebanon and the British in Jordan. Indeed, it was alleged that the Russians also had an invitation from some sort of Hungarian government just as we had from Middle Eastern governments. The comparison is unfair but plausible to many Asian ears. It is one more reason for a policy of military disengagement in the Middle East.

Military disengagement as an American policy must be part of a constructive program looking to general peace and prosperity in the lands which saw the birth of civilization. Underlying that policy should be certain basic principles and policies which I should list as follows:

(1) Recognition that the military neutralization of the Middle East rather than any attempt to involve any or all of its nations on our side in a cold war is not only a good in itself, but all that America can hope for, at least in the Arab world. The attempt for more plays into the hands of the USSR. Military neutralization may be served by a UN guarantee of borders but not by unilateral guarantees by one or another of the Big Powers. The psychological effect of the well-intentioned Eisenhower Doctrine was bad; the Baghdad Pact was worse, and Mr. Dulles' haste to underwrite it by firmer American commitments after the Iraqi revolution was a grave disservice to peace in the Middle East and the whole world.

(2) Military neutralization of the Middle East requires a definite agreement with the Soviet Union. To achieve it will be difficult but no one can say that it is impossible until our government has tried with an earnestness of effort quite opposite to its failure even to examine the Bulganin note which we have quoted. There is evidence that Khrushchev for his own sake wants peace. He may be at least as ready as we to rely on advancing his cause by ideological and economic competition. He would probably agree that an arms race in the Middle East threatens world peace at least as much as a continuance of tests of nuclear weapons. He has let his scientists agree objectively with ours on the sort of inspection which will guarantee agreements on discontinuance of tests and on the problems of safe, peaceful use of nuclear energy. Why

not a somewhat similar meeting of minds on the objective conditions of peace in the Middle East?

(3) Military demilitarization in the Middle East means disarmament, which even Ben-Gurion theoretically favors. But he and the Arab leaders will probably resist the action of big powers in forcing an arms embargo on them unless as part of a general program of disarmament in which the big powers share. Here is a striking illustration of the necessity of tying in disengagement with disarmament.

(4) It is the United Nations which must be the effective agency for security in the Middle East. Backed by both sides in the cold war, it should guarantee boundaries in the Middle East against change by external aggression. It should use its weight against the kind of "indirect aggression" exemplified by broadcasting stations in one country overtly advocating violence in another. But indirect aggression can scarcely be policed by force, and great care should be taken lest any action against indirect aggression become an attempt to suppress free discussion of world problems. (My guess is that some of my own occasional remarks over the Voice of America, Radio Free Europe, and Radio Liberation, although I have carefully eschewed any advocacy of violence, might be judged by dictators to be indirect aggression.)

(5) Both the United States and the United Nations should welcome progress in Arab unity, achieved without aggressive violence, as likely to constitute a valuable balance in tomorrow's world. The United States cannot continually equate its interest in the independence of na-

tions with alliances with autocrats like King Saud. It must respect the right of revolution to which it owes its own existence. There will be plenty of internal difficulties to be overcome before achieving a sound and viable Arab unity, organic or federated. Bourguiba of Tunisia has shown resentment against any sort of dictation from Egypt and commendably has every intention of preserving his independence. But it is not the business of the West to create Arab divisions for its own ends.

(6) The United States should be ready to make good its promise (or boasts) of help in setting up the cooperative regional authorities in the Middle East to deal with the problems of oil, water, and credit. One possible plan was suggested by a group of independent British Middle East experts. It is thus described by James P. Warburg in *Agenda for Action*:

"The basic assumption of this group was that there could be no security from expropriation of foreign-owned oil installations and no security against sabotage of pipelines controlled by private oil companies, unless foreign development of oil resources acquired the firm backing of Middle Eastern public opinion and recognized international law. The group put forward substantially the following proposal:

"It suggested that by international agreement a United Nations Regional Development Authority be authorized to place a levy upon all oil shipments from Middle Eastern ports, and that, in addition, the Development Authority should take over and operate all Middle East pipelines, charging an additional levy to cover operating costs and

existing charges for transit rights. The proceeds from both
levies would then be contributed toward an approved economic development program for the entire area.

"By this means, the authors of the plan contended
that the oil companies and the oil consumers would obtain greatly increased and internationally guaranteed security of operation. They would, admittedly, pay more for
Middle Eastern oil than they had been paying, but 'not as
much as it will certainly cost them if Middle East conditions continue as anarchic as they otherwise must become.' "

What makes the adoption of some such program as I
have outlined peculiarly difficult is the seemingly implacable Arab hate for Israel, a hatred which Israel has
done little to assuage. Here the West, especially the United
States, bears a peculiar responsibility. There is great force
in the Arab contention that Jews were never persecuted
under Islam as under Christianity; that Hitler was not an
Arab, and that when his attempt to exterminate the Jews
within his reach made some refuge for them essential the
United States did not open wide its doors but expected the
Arabs by their hospitality to pay for Christian crimes.
Israel has been and is to a very large extent the beneficiary
of support from the American government as well as of
the generosity of American Jews. Arab states, they say,
have had no comparable aid.

Many Arabs of importance have indicated that they
would come to peaceful terms with Israel on three conditions often implied rather than clearly stated: (1) that

Israel withdraw to the boundaries of the UN partition plan; (2) that it take no more Jewish immigrants, at least until after (3) it repatriates all Arab refugees.

This, I think, is an impossible program which the Israeli cannot be expected to accept. The boundaries set by the UN were scarcely boundaries of a viable state, yet it was the Arab states, not Israel, which rejected the whole partition plan and took up arms against it. Having appealed to the stern arbitrament of war, they lost. In ten years history has moved fast. Israel, in its present boundaries fixed by the armistice, is a progressive and homogeneous state. To cut off any of its present territory would be to answer tragedy by tragedy and give us new refugees for old. What adjustments of boundaries should be made— and they are many—should be made by negotiation involving no substantial change in Israel's area.

Repatriation of Arab refugees is a moral right. It should be recognized as such, and substitutes for it should be offered in the light of that recognition. If Israel can support anything like the Jewish population which I was told it can certainly provide for, it must physically have rooms for more Arabs than heretofore Ben-Gurion has offered to receive under any circumstances. It would, however, be badly swamped by an influx of all refugees, and its security perhaps imperiled even if they all took oaths of allegiance. In spite of the refugees' protestations, I doubt if all of them would want to return to a homeland as profoundly changed as is Israel, especially since Syria and Iraq are underpopulated.

It is late in the day to work out any bi-national plan

such as Dr. Magnes proposed. Practically, the best that can be done would seem to be a recognition of the moral right of the refugees to their former property with an offer of a larger quota of returnees than has yet been suggested and much greater indemnification for the rest, not only on the basis of compensation for property but for the years of imposed idleness without any return for expropriated lands and homes. Here the United States, not as a charity, but as a duty, should contribute what Israel may not be able to provide, since the United States has been deeply involved in the establishment and maintenance of Israel as a sanctuary for Jewish refugees who are excluded (as are the Arab refugees) from American territory by American immigration laws. Resettlement should be under a UN authority.

For Israel to refuse to receive any more Jewish immigrants would be to deny its purpose of existence. But Arab fears of Israeli expansion as "the spearhead of a new Western colonialism," while exaggerated, have some basis which Israel should try hard to remove. The second largest party in Israel today is definitely expansionist. Ben-Gurion's own occasional utterances, his insistence that the Diaspora—that is, the Jews outside Israel—should someday return, his efforts to stimulate mass immigration, all made it logical for Arabs to fear what prominent leaders told me they feared, an effort by the brave and well-trained Israeli army to act for expansion. It would be backed (as in the Suez affair) by the French and the British with American sympathy and support. "Ridiculous," many Jews have sincerely told me. Definitely so in this

extreme form, but then why not say so? Let Israel and the
Zionist movement disclaim any attempt at forcible expansion, any desire to constrain *all* Jews to come in, and Arabs
might sooner reconcile themselves to the fact of Israel's
existence and the possibility that she might make a helpful
and cooperative neighbor. They might stop drawing his-
torical parallels between Israel and the Latin Kingdom
founded and maintained by the Crusaders for more than
a century, but now long since vanished without political
trace.

It was bad business that the UN, backed by the
United States, failed utterly in such attempts as it made
to turn Ralph Bunche's armistice into a peace. The years
have made the task harder. It must be undertaken, and
every practicable moral pressure and economic induce-
ment be put upon the Arab states and Israel to negotiate
true peace.

Such efforts to bring about Arab-Israeli peace should
be added to the six principles and policies set forth on pp.
129–131 in order to implement a constructive disengagement of the United States in the Middle East. Our own
peace and the world's is jeopardized by the vaguely understood but strong commitments which make it possible for
other nations—for instance, in the Baghdad Pact—to
plunge us into war on the very borders of the Soviet
Union.

IX.

Disengagement: Middle Europe

WHEN THE UNITED STATES entered World War II
the last thing it wanted was empire. Its people sought
peace with security, which they somewhat naively assumed
would be achieved with the elimination of Hitler and
Nazism. None of us imagined that in the year 1958 American troops would be stationed in Europe, and that America
would assume the principal obligation of the defense of
fourteen sovereign nations, loosely united in the North
Atlantic Treaty Organization, against attack from their
and our former ally, the Soviet Union, under conditions
where almost any one of them would have power to plunge
us into war.

This is not the place to tell in detail how the present
situation emerged out of total military victory over that
arch-enemy of mankind, Nazism. But it is important for
our purpose to understand that it is not adequately ex-

plained simply and solely in terms of Stalin's implacable drive for power for the new Russian Communist imperialism. Behind it lies also the fact that war doesn't end war; that its inescapable devastation, spiritual as well as physical, cripples the understanding and moral insights on which abiding peace depends.

World War I climaxed Europe's effort to organize its life in terms of the economics of private capitalism and the politics of fanatic competitive nationalisms of sovereign states of unequal power. A few great powers established imperial control over vast areas of industrially underdeveloped Asia and Africa. The complete military victory of "democracy" shook but did not destroy the old systems of capitalist imperialism. After Versailles there emerged no federated Europe for which commonsense cried out, nor any League of Nations strong enough to curb and guide the violent forces, new and old, which led to World War II. So exhausting was that war that the real wonder is that an exhausted Western Europe recovered as well as it did. American aid, wisely and generously given, helped mightily in the process. But our leaders' wartime approach to peace and European reorganization through the negative doctrine of "unconditional surrender"; an extravagant fear in high quarters that Stalin, crossed, might make a separate peace with Hitler; mixed with unwarranted hope in his continued cooperation; followed by the nationalist revolts against European empire, laid an impossible foundation for the secure peace of our dreams.

At war's end, American troops had precipitately been brought home, leaving what we now call the satellite states: Poland, Hungary, Czechoslovakia, Rumania, Bulgaria, and Albania within Stalin's grasp. Germany was partitioned for administrative purposes and Berlin was left an island in a Russian or Communist sea. By the end of 1949 in answer to the Communist coup in Czechoslovakia and the Russian blockade of Berlin, NATO was formed, and first West and then East Germany were set up as states by the respective occupying powers. In 1950 the Korean war was begun by Communist aggression and Secretary Acheson demanded a drastic increase in European rearmament and inclusion of a German contingent in NATO. American troops were in Europe to stay, and Washington was committed to expend Americans in a deterrent action against Russia all the way up to the iron curtain. The keystone of the Acheson policy, followed in this respect by Mr. Dulles, was support of NATO and German rearmament. Neither pushed with imagination or determination for a general disarmament of which the establishment of a demilitarized zone in Central Europe might well have been one phase or one beginning. The one breach in this program of militarization and more militarization was the final peace treaty with Austria, eight years in the making, which successfully neutralized and demilitarized that little country.

As for NATO, by 1952 Greece and Turkey were added to protect its Mediterranean flank against invasion and a high goal of ninety divisions was set for the alliance. In 1954, when this goal seemed unattainable, the fateful decision was reached to offset deficiency of manpower by equipping NATO defense forces with tactical weapons in which we assumed that the United States had so great a superiority that thus armed, thirty divisions might thrust back any invasion. What happened next, James P. Warburg in his *Agenda for Action* thus describes with critical comment on it:

"But even the 30 divisions never materialized. Whereas, in 1949, Western Europe had 12 divisions available for NATO, in February 1957, Western Europe was providing less than 6 divisions for its own defense. Apart from 5 American and 4 British divisions, there were available to NATO: 1 Canadian-Danish division, 3 undermanned Belgian divisions, 1 Dutch division and 1 French training division, the rest of the French army being in North Africa. As for the Mediterranean flank, it had all but disintegrated, due chiefly to the Anglo-Greek-Turkish quarrel over Cyprus.

"Six years after the United States had demanded West German rearmament, there was not a single German division in the field; but the decision to remilitarize Germany had shaken the morale of Western Europe, exacerbated East-West tensions and left a partitioned Germany ticking like a time-bomb in the heart of the European Continent. This threat to peace could hardly be expected to diminish when a streamlined, professional German army, equipped with atomic weapons would finally take the field.

"What had this painful 8-year effort to build a shield accomplished? Could anyone believe that the pitifully small NATO forces, even if fully equipped with atomic weapons, could do anything more than bravely fight a

brief delaying action? Could anyone believe that much
would be left of Western Europe after that delaying action
had been fought?

"The simple fact which our government had all along
refused to recognize was that, after the overhasty de-
mobilization at the conclusion of World War II, there
never has been a way to make Western Europe safe against
Russian invasion, except by preventing that invasion from
being attempted."

It was and is extraordinarily unlikely that the third
world war will come by a cold-blooded Russian invasion
of Western Europe. If it begins in Europe it will far more
probably come (1) out of some accident or incident where
armed forces continually confront each other, (2) out of
a possible German drive for reunification, or some internal
revolt which will draw in outside armies, or (3) a sudden
decision of a Russian dictator who thinks himself temporarily possessed of great superiority of missiles to use the
opportunity for presenting an ultimatum to the United
States and its allies: let them submit or he will stage a
sudden, direct attack on the United States and its important bases in Europe. Conceivably, but doubtfully, he
might attack without a previous ultimatum.

Again I agree with James P. Warburg's judgment on
the nature of the Communist danger:

"The Russian threat was and to a certain extent still
is a threat of political subversion—a threat which has been
greatly reduced by the restoration of Western Europe's
economic health and political stability through Marshall

Plan aid. But, even if one assumes that the intention to invade did at some time exist, the fact remains that it was never executed, either before NATO came into existence or later, when French involvement in colonial wars and German delay in rearming created the most inviting opportunities. If the intention existed, the deterrent was provided not by the wholly inadequate conventional forces in Western Europe but by the certain knowledge that an attack upon an almost defenseless Western Europe would bring on World War III, with the United States ranged against the Soviet Union. The Russians know that in such a war there could be no such thing as victory. They are also only too well aware that their purposes are better served by continuing to fish in the troubled waters of an uneasy peace.

"There was one possible explanation for the fateful American decision, in 1949, to undertake the erection of a shield against the invasion of Western Europe; namely, to bolster European morale and to create the will to resist. If such was, indeed, the reason for the undertaking, its purpose was defeated by the psychological effect of the decision to rearm Germany."

It is impossible to see how there can be a final and generally acceptable peace in Europe with Germany divided. It is equally impossible to see how either side, ours or the Russian, can consent to a reunited armed Germany in the camp of the other. Yet this is what the West has been demanding for itself and Germany. Mr. Dulles took occasion to state that demand, endorsed by the United States, Great Britain, France, and West Germany in the summer of 1957, regardless of its effect on the disarmament discussions in London, presumably to help bring about the re-election of Chancellor Adenauer.

Some of my German Socialist friends insist that the Chancellor and other powerful people in the German political and economic setup do not really care for German unity. The Chancellor is a Roman Catholic who in his youth was a Rhinelander separationist. What is now East Germany is or was the area of greatest Protestant strength. West Germany has rather remarkably resettled millions of Germans not only from East Germany but the former German territories appropriated by the Poles. They are doing well enough without war. Every year that passes makes it harder easily to integrate the differing economies of the two Germanys. There is, moreover, always a chance that in a reunited Germany Eastern Germans might discover and present some old shares of stocks giving unwelcome claims on great West German corporations long since reorganized.

Nevertheless, however lukewarm may be the desire of powerful groups to put words into action, no German party dares to renounce the demand for unity. Unsatisfied, that will be a demand with which parties and rulers can play. It breeds the kind of nationalist feeling that in our age has proved so powerful a force for evil as well as good. One can easily imagine circumstances under which a future German government would wreck Western alliances and imperil Europe by a deal with Russia for German unity.

At present it seems utopian to think that Moscow or the Communist movement would consent to reunion at all except on Communist terms, which at the very least would demand negotiation by two sovereign governments rather than a free election by all the German people. A demilitarized Germany would not automatically and immediately become a reunited Germany. It would make unity far more likely of attainment. Without demilitarization there certainly will not be peaceful reunification, and the lack of it will be a prime factor in building up again a military spirit in the truncated nation whose recovery of economic and social strength is a postwar marvel. If there are cosmic observers of the human drama on this small earthly stage how must they regard the cosmic jest which sees us so deeply concerned to build up the military power not only of Germany but of Japan after we had destroyed them at so great a price!

What gives hope that the Soviet Union would agree to extending the area of demilitarization begun in Austria is the dramatic evidence provided by East German revolt in 1953 and Polish revolt in 1956, quickly followed by revolution in Hungary, which was only crushed by the intervention of Russian arms and Russian military occupation. Clearly the satellites are military liabilities rather than assets to the USSR. Economically they can no longer be so easily milked for the Communist stepmotherland as formerly. Hence Moscow's willingness to talk some degree of demilitarization. Poland's foreign minister, Rapacki, never could have proposed his plan in 1957 without Moscow's blessing.

To that plan we shall return after we have reviewed the renewed interest in a demilitarized Middle European area which has been manifest among the peoples if not the governments of the West. George Kennan, principal author of the original theory of Communist containment, gave the interest eloquent expression in his much discussed series of addresses, *Russia, the Atom, and the West,* over the British Broadcasting Corporation in 1957. He held that if Western continental countries are to be armed with nuclear weapons—and they are, whatever happens to further tests—any Russian withdrawal from Central and Eastern Europe "may become unthinkable once and for all, for reasons of sheer military prudence regardless of what the major Western powers might be prepared to do." Mr. Kennan continued:

"Is there, then, any reasonably hopeful alternative to the unpromising path along which we are now advancing? I must confess that I see only one. This is precisely the opposite of the attempt to incorporate the tactical atomic weapon into the defense of Western Europe. It is, again, the possibility of separating geographically the forces of the great nuclear powers, of excluding them as direct factors in the future development of political relationships on the Continent, and of inducing the continental peoples, by the same token, to accept a higher level of responsibility for the defense of the Continent than they have recently borne. This is still a possibility. Close as we are to it, we have not yet taken the fatal step. The continental countries have not yet prejudiced their usefulness for the solution of continental problems, as we have ours, by building their defense establishments around the atomic weapon. If they could be induced to refrain from doing this, and if there could be a general withdrawal of American, British and Russian armed power from the heart of the Continent, there would be at least a chance that Europe's fortunes might be worked out, and the competition between two political philosophies carried forward, in a manner disastrous neither to the respective peoples themselves nor to the cause of world peace. I would not know where else this chance is to be looked for."

Mr. Kennan did not elaborate his suggestion into a detailed plan. He admitted that "if this [military defense] were the problem, then of course foreign assistance would be needed, although it is questionable whether it could ever be enough."

"But this is not the problem. We must get over this obsession that the Russians are yearning to attack and occupy Western Europe, and that this is the principal danger. The Soviet threat, as I have had occasion to say before, is a combined military and political threat, with the accent on the political. If the armed forces of the United States and Britain were not present on the Continent, the problem of defense for the continental nations would be primarily one of the internal health and discipline of the respective national societies, and of the manner in which they were organized to prevent the conquest and subjugation of their national life by unscrupulous and foreign-inspired minorities in their midst. What they need is a strategic doctrine addressed to this reality. Under such a doctrine, armed forces would indeed be needed; but I would suggest that as a general rule these forces might better be paramilitary ones, of a territorial-militia type, somewhat on the Swiss example, rather than regular military units on the World War II pattern."

In opposing Mr. Kennan's theories Messrs. Acheson and Dulles found their hearts beating as one. From a very different position than theirs I should argue that Mr. Kennan's doubts about working for general disarmament until specific political problems are solved weakens his argument for disengagement requiring so high a measure of disarmament in Middle Europe. Regional disarmament alone will not by any means solve the specific political problems responsible for the cold war. It has been hard for the West to start Germany to rearming. It may be far harder to make her, a sovereign nation, accept the Kennan proposal unless as part of a valuable step toward, or condition of, general disarmament.

Poland's foreign minister, Rapacki, was more specific in his formal proposal of atomic disarmament in Middle Europe. In its official form it applied only to nuclear weapons of all sorts and seemed to me open to grave objection, first, because on our side and presumably the Russian, nuclear weapons are rapidly becoming conventional, and a sweeping prohibition of them very hard to inspect and enforce; and, second, because atomic disarmament would leave untouched and more decisive the East's superiority in manpower. But I had an opportunity to hear Mr. Rapacki explain his plan unofficially when he attended the Special Session of the UN's Assembly in Aug., 1958.

As I understood him he would gladly couple it with large specific reductions of all armed forces and consider it a phase in general disarmament. Western governments in earnest about peace would even now explore this plan rather than reject it out of hand. No sympathy with forces for "liberation" in satellite states should lead us to believe that they would be strengthened by our insistence on NATO's confronting the iron curtain with atom bombs in its hands. The kind of war that this sort of engagement makes probable would liberate only desolation.*

In December 1956 an Arden House Conference on Disarmament unanimously accepted a memorandum on possible immediate steps prepared by a subcommittee chaired by Mr. Warburg for presentation to President Eisenhower containing this paragraph:

"After consulting its allies, it seems to us that the U. S. government might say that it looks with favor upon the proposal for eventual complete withdrawal of Soviet, British and American forces from all continental Europe West of the Soviet frontier but that it considers that such a withdrawal can be accomplished only by a careful step-wise procedure. The first step in such a procedure might well be the withdrawal of NATO forces to the West bank of the Rhine and the withdrawal of Soviet forces to the Oder-Western Neisse rivers with suitable arrangements

* On Nov. 7, 1958, after this chapter was written, Mr. Rapacki submitted a revised and more comprehensive version of his plan which might well be made the basis of negotiation. If the West would negotiate on this basis and formally recognize the Oder-Neisse line as the boundary between Germany and Poland, it might provide a framework for a fair and peaceful solution of the Berlin crisis.

for air and ground inspection. These arrangements might include Soviet control posts, including a radar screen, on the East bank of the Rhine, and Western control posts, including a radar screen, on the West bank of the Oder-Neisse. Suitable arrangements would, of course, have to be made for the preservation of the status quo in Berlin."

The setting for such a proposal is now somewhat different than it was at the end of 1956. If plans for inspecting the abolition of nuclear tests go well it would make easier an extension of inspection to cover mutual troop withdrawals. Once we feel compelled to accept the notion that in our kind of world progress toward secure peace must be made step by step rather than by any conceivable leap to security, the phased withdrawal of troops in Central Europe becomes a necessary part of the process of disarmament and disengagement.

That constructive idea will have to come from outside NATO's councils. Efforts to make that organization anything more than a rather shaky military alliance have come to almost nothing. NATO has played no role toward European economic or political federation; it has not promoted peace in the dangerous North African area, but merely made it possible for France to withdraw troops and planes from Europe to fight her war. Some of the most troublesome quarrels in the European area involve NATO members as antagonists; Britain, Greece, and Turkey over Cyprus; Britain and Iceland over fishing rights. Clearly, Europe isn't going to be saved merely by a military alliance inspired solely by fear of the Soviet Union. And we Americans can't save her by involving ourselves in a mere increase of military strength. We should instead seek a demilitarized zone in Central Europe. That would be consistent with an obligation to protect a democratic West Berlin which cannot be made forever secure simply by perpetuating the status quo.

X.

Strengthening the United Nations

BETWEEN NAPOLEON'S downfall and the outbreak of World War I there were comparatively stable arrangements and understandings making it possible for men and nations to live in an ordered if not a well ordered world. The doctrine of the absolute sovereignty of nations, large and small, was accepted, but in practice a few imperial systems dominated millions of Asians and Africans. The Monroe Docrine protected the Latin American states. Between empires an uneasy peace, or at least absence of total war, was maintained by balance of power until the grim logic of competitive capitalist imperialism and rival military preparedness suddenly plunged them into a stupid and brutal war. Before that conflict, thanks to the widespread gold standard and the absence of quotas and bureaucratic controls, there was a freedom of trade and travel unknown since our victorious wars to make the world safe for democracy. (I traveled rather extensively in Asia, including Japan, Korea, and China in 1906–1907 while discontent ran high in Korea, but I never had to show my passport once, a fact I remembered as almost Utopian on my travels in 1951 and afterwards.)

There was another force making for genuine internationalism and peace before the cataclysm of 1914. That was democratic socialism, to whose adherents the brotherhood of the workers of the world was a tremendous emotional reality. But nothing had been done before the war to plan to put that emotion into effective antimobilization activities on both sides of the line of impending conflict. Very soon socialists were killing socialists as cheerfully, or docilely, as Christians were killing Christians. Democratic Socialism in 1914 missed a tremendous opportunity of a sort which never could return again.

For what it destroyed and the passions of divisive nationalism which it fanned, World War I offered the League of Nations by way of compensation in approach to peace and order. After a history of very moderate usefulness, it fell victim to Hitler.

There was never much doubt in the minds of the architects of victory in World War II that the League must have a successor and a successor strong enough to prevent new imperial systems from rushing into vacuums of power created by the war itself and the turbulence of the postwar world in which the days of the old empires of even the victors were clearly numbered. From that war only two very great powers emerged, the USA and the USSR, the latter driven by the demon of Communist expansion.

Otherwise nationalism or the passion for it was a mightier and more divisive force than ever before.

Under the circumstances, it was the successful establishment of the United Nations rather than its obvious imperfection which invites our wonder. In approaching victory and what to do with it the Allied leaders in the West, especially Roosevelt, gambled on being able to hold together the allies in war for the establishment of peace. That gamble was manifest in the Charter of the United Nations and the composition of the Security Council, to which much power was given. It was clearly advisable to include one of the great or potentially great Asian nations in the group of nations possessed of a veto power. Japan was a defeated enemy; India was not yet independent; so the lot fell on Chiang Kai-shek's China which, it was hoped, would emerge in strength after the war. Hope lies in the fact that the UN lived, although the Roosevelt gamble of continuing allied cooperation was lost.

The advent of the UN was observed with general interest and approval which continues and even seems to be gaining, but the young organization has nowhere evoked the intense loyalties called out by desire for national independence and the passions of Communism and anti-Communism. It has had no sense of world citizenship on which to call comparable to the feeling on which even corrupt and tyrannical national governments can rely.

Yet it has a record of worthwhile success in peculiarly difficult years. Thus our State Department summarizes it:

"By its action the United Nations: played a major role in the withdrawal of Soviet troops from Iran in 1946 . . .

helped bring to an end the Communist war in Greece . . . condemned the Chinese Communists as aggressors in Korea and fought to roll back aggression there . . . brought about a truce between India and Pakistan in Kashmir . . . avoided a major war in the Suez crisis by bringing the pressure of world opinion to bear for a quick end to hostilities . . . condemned the Soviet Union's invasion of Hungary and revealed its brutal repression of the Hungarian people's efforts to achieve freedom . . . cleared the Suez Canal and reopened it to the commerce of the world . . . created an International Atomic Energy Agency for the peaceful development of the atom . . . has fought poverty, hunger, disease, and ignorance in many lands in order to improve the general well-being of mankind and remove some of the basic causes of war."

To this must now be added the conspicuous success of the Assembly in ending the *immediate* crisis in the Middle East which led to the landing of American troops in Lebanon and British in Jordan. Elsewhere the State Department document which I have quoted refers to the usefulness of the United Nations Emergency Force in preserving order along the border of the Gaza Strip and thus maintaining the cease-fire order.

This record hardly tells the whole story. The UN could not have stopped hostilities in the Suez except for the unity of the USA and the USSR on this one matter. It was a similar unity at an earlier date which enabled the UN to recognize the new state of Israel, and through the effective work of Ralph Bunche, finally to bring about an armistice in the Arab-Israel war. It has never been able to turn that armistice into peace or to substitute agreed peace for the unquiet truce between India and Pakistan. Its long discussions of disarmament have until now done nothing concrete to check or abate the monstrous armed race to death.

In other words, in its primary business of keeping peace and promoting disarmament, the UN's usefulness has been more as an instrument of the US and its allies, or —as in the Suez crisis—the US and the Soviet Union than as an independent international authority. For its good work in fighting "poverty, hunger, disease and ignorance in many lands" it has had far less money than the US and the USSR have spent on similar efforts under conditions which too often have made their benevolence merely a factor in the cold war.

The reasons for the weaknesses of the UN are two, and are closely related. It has not the proper degree of support among either the governments or peoples of the world, and its constitutional machinery is inadequate to its major job of maintaining peace by the substitution of law for war.

Almost from the UN's beginning there have been two different and well-supported approaches to more adequate international organization. One, in its more uncompromising form, sought nothing less than full world government on a federal basis, like that of the United States or more probably Switzerland. It dealt not too specifically with abstract considerations of governmental machinery for ruling mankind. Its advocacy was an intellectual exercise not without value unless pressed as an immediate political program. The other approach accepted the imperfect UN and sought to strengthen it, less by abstract discussion of an ideal federal government of mankind than by pragmatic reforms essential to the implementation of universal disarmament.

In the short period before the cold war became the supreme international reality I discussed international organization on several platforms with an eloquent and dedicated advocate of World Government *now*. I saw him lose large groups of his auditors, not because of too narrow a patriotism, of which there was plenty in evidence, but of fear of anything so vast and centralized as any world government would become, assuming that by some impossible miracle it could be achieved. Under such all-embracing rule of peoples of very different degrees and types of development, there might develop a tyranny of imposed conformity, a world without cities of refuge for diversity and freedom. There is in our time not even the minimum common denominator of culture, economic development, and traditional loyalties which would make possible anything like what mankind associates with the word "government" on a worldwide scale. It could only be imposed and maintained by overpowering force. In short, this absolutist approach to a complete world government, even of a federal type, seemed to me as undesirable as it was politically impractical.

To my mind the proper approach was and is the best possible use of the UN and its agencies, with insistence upon the necessity of general disarmament as a condition of man's existence and hence insistence upon the changes necessary to make the UN the instrument in achieving it. We should seek minimum rather than maximum changes in the existing Charter, provided that a specific change is adequate to our immediate purpose, and that no change should be considered as final in a developing world society with need of increasing federal cooperation. Some strength could be added to the UN without changes in the Charter. For example, Attorney General William P. Rogers, to his credit, has urged that the United States re-examine its present insistence upon the right to determine whether the World Court trespasses upon domestic jurisdiction. The Court's domain in international affairs is now, he argued, tragically limited.

There have been many good studies of possible changes in the UN by amendments to its Charter. The one that I have found most provocative and satisfactory is *World Peace through World Law* by Grenville Clark and Louis Sohn. Years of work went into its preparation. It was published in its final form by the Harvard University Press early in 1958. One great merit of the book is that it has carefully stated the reasons leading the authors to their specific proposals and then has examined objections to them. The result is a rational plan, in which the reader may differ from some proposals, but if he is fair-minded he must put his reasons for difference on an equally rational basis rather than rejecting changes on the basis of prejudice or emotion. While the plan is closely knit and therefore it and possible amendments to it would be better considered as a whole, many of its suggestions might be adopted piece-meal. If progress in strengthening the UN must come that way, it will nevertheless be immensely advantageous to have this comprehensive view of what could be done held steadily before the eyes of the friends and supporters of the UN in and out of public office.

We have lived through enough years to know that the alternatives to a strengthened UN are (a) further growth of a competitive new imperialism of the giant powers; or (b) an intolerable anarchy of some ninety-three nations now generally recognized or likely soon to be recognized as independent and sovereign. These legally equal sovereign states range in population from China, with 615,-000,000 inhabitants, to Iceland, with 160,000. In wealth, resources, and military power, actual and potential, they range from the USA and the USSR to Albania or Jordan or Libya. The UN, if it is to offer a third alternative to empire or to anarchy and war, must be strengthened. To some extent that can be done within the framework of the present Charter. It cannot be adequately done without a better system of representation, better formal machinery for dealing with disputes, and a feasible plan of enforcing the decisions and agreements upon which peace depends. Only thus can law become the substitute for war. The UN today lacks constitutional power to go far in providing or enforcing law. But the volume of appropriate law must be limited to that necessary for the preservation of peace. Mr. Clark states thus the approach to the problem of limitation:

"The powers of the world organization should be restricted to matters directly related to the maintenance of peace. All other powers should be reserved to the nations and their peoples. This definition and reservation of powers is advisable not only to avoid opposition based on fear of possible interference in the domestic affairs of the nations, but also because it is wise for this generation to limit itself to the single task of preventing international violence or the threat of it. If we can accomplish that we should feel satisfied and could well leave to later generations any enlargement of the powers of the world organization that they might find desirable."

Earlier, Mr. Clark had written: "The following are the basic principles by which Professor Sohn and I have been governed.

"*First:* It is futile to expect genuine peace until there is put into effect an effective system of enforceable world law in the limited field of war prevention. This implies the adoption on a world-wide basis of the measures and institutions which the experience of centuries has shown to be essential for the maintenance of law and order, namely, clearly stated law against violence, courts to interpret and apply that law, and police to enforce it. All else, we conceive, depends upon the acceptance of this approach.

"*Second:* The world law against international violence must be explicitly stated in constitutional and statutory form and must, under appropriate penalties, forbid the use of force by any nation against any other for any cause whatever, save only in self-defense.

"*Third:* World judicial tribunals to interpret and apply the world law against international violence must be established and maintained, and also organization and adjustment in place of violence, or the threat of it, as a means of dealing with international disputes.

"*Fourth:* A permanent world police force must be

created and maintained which, while safeguarded with utmost care against misuse, would be fully adequate to forestall or suppress any violation of the world law against international violence.

"*Fifth:* The complete disarmament of all the nations (rather than the 'reduction' or 'limitation' of armaments) is essential, this disarmament to be accomplished in a simultaneous and proportionate manner by carefully verified stages and subject to a well-organized system of inspection. It is now generally accepted that disarmament must be universal and enforceable. That it must also be complete is no less necessary, since; (a) in the nuclear age no mere reduction in the new means of mass destruction could be effective to remove fear and tension; and (b) if any substantial national armaments were to remain, even if only ten percent of the armaments of 1957–58, it would be impracticable to maintain a sufficiently strong world police force to deal with any possible aggression or revolt against the authority of the world organization. We should face the fact that until there is complete disarmament under world law there can be no assurance of genuine peace.

"*Sixth:* Effective world machinery must be created to mitigate the vast disparities in the economic condition of various regions of the world, the continuance of which tends to instability and conflict."

It lies beyond the scope of this brief book to summarize the entire Clark-Sohn Plan. Here I must content myself by giving some of the authors' answers to questions always asked of Charter revisionists. They would abolish the Security Council and substitute for it an Executive Committee of a strengthened General Assembly. The latter would be composed as follows:

"All nations recognized as independent states and which are, therefore, eligible for membership, would be divided into seven categories according to population. Their representation (including five nations which as of July 1957 were not yet recognized as independent states but are likely to be so recognized within a few years) would be as follows on the basis of estimated populations as of July 1, 1957:"

Over 140 million	4 nations	30 Representatives	120
40–140 million	8 nations	16 Representatives	128
20–40 million	11 nations	8 Representatives	88
5–20 million	35 nations	5 Representatives	175
1.5–5 million	23 nations	3 Representatives	69
0.5–1.5 million	10 nations	2 Representatives	20
Under 0.5 million	2 nations	1 Representative	2

Representatives should vote as individuals. In budget legislation some protection is given the nations which would have to finance appropriations by the following provision: "All decisions of the General Assembly pursuant to this Article shall be made by a majority of all the Representatives then in office, whether or not present and voting, including in respect of votes on the adoption of the budgets of the United Nations a majority of the Representatives then in office, whether or not present and voting, from the member Nations which would have the ten largest quotas of the budget then voted upon."

The principal organs of the United Nations beside the General Assembly and the Executive Council would be, as today, Economic and Social Council, a Trusteeship Council, an International Court of Justice, and a Secretariat, to which would be added a World Equity Tribunal and a World Conciliation Board, whose functions the authors carefully define. They propose also a World Development Authority to which we shall refer in discussing the economics of peace.

It would be absurd to say that the strengthening of the United Nations, upon which peace depends, requires an acceptance of the Clark-Sohn plan and a refusal to consider any alternative. There are details in it which I should question. It is obvious that neither that plan nor any alternative can be achieved without a great awakening of the peoples of the world to the necessity for an international agency of law and its enforcement as a condition of a secure peace. But such an awakening will be made more probable and more purposeful if not only are the reasons for strengthening the United Nations held before us, but also a concrete plan is offered to guide and stimulate our thinking. The sharpest critics of the Clark-Sohn book are basically skeptics not merely of a particular plan but of any disarmament under a strengthened UN. That skepticism rests upon an almost total denial of rationality to man. It would condemn us or our posterity to the death inherent in a stubborn preference for war over law in the age of nuclear weapons. The troubled history of our human race is nevertheless a history of enough achievement to warrant emphatic rejection of so dire an inevitability.

XI.

The Economics of Peace

A CELESTIAL VISITOR from some distant star (provided his world is not as crazy as ours) would be greatly surprised at the extraordinary differences in standards of living and mastery of technical devices among the "sovereign" nations into which we earthlings are divided. He would discover a per capita gross national product of $2500 in the United States and about $80 in India and Pakistan. He might pick up a notable book, *The Affluent Society*, and learn how in the United States the extraordinary actual and potential productivity of modern technology had made the conventional, traditional wisdom inapplicable, and the exhortations of that wisdom to steady, though ill-requited, toil as the condition of existence misleading. He would find here a society which keeps going by persuading people under high pressure to want what they didn't know they needed. But outside of the United States and certain other areas holding a minority of the world's population he would find some two billion people so far below

162

the Western standard of living that flood, drought, or natural disaster can push them over the thin line which separates hunger from starvation.

Moreover, despite the efforts of industrially backward nations to possess themselves of modern machinery and the appropriate skills, and some economic aid from the more prosperous nations, the gap is widening, not narrowing. The popular saying, "them as has, gits," as Gunnar Myrdal has pointed out, is being fulfilled before our eyes.

It must, of course, be added that in all countries, rich or poor, there is a more or less unjust economic inequality between classes. Poor India's rich ex-rajahs are among the world's wealthiest men. But in awakening nations there seems to be a present tendency for the resentment of the poor to be directed along national lines against wealthier nations to the great hurt of a fraternal peace.

Our celestial visitor, if we may go back to him, would not be surprised to find these enormous disparities a major cause of the unrest which menaces the world's peace. He might be more surprised to discover that the issues over which men in this present time are likely to fight are, on the face of them, national. In arguing for a worldwide attack on bitter and unnecessary poverty we are not falling back on the famous but inaccurate cry, "Workers of the world, unite; you have nothing to lose but your chains. You have a world to gain." That slogan has had little practical success in uniting the workers across national lines partly because there is such a difference in the weight and character of the chains, and partly because of the inevitable psychological results of our nationalist and cultural divisions. History and current events furnish plenty of evidence that men are as willing to kill or to die for their power and their prejudices as for their property, for what they call their principles as for their profits. The dictates of prejudice and economic interest usually, but by no means always, coincide.

We men are greatly conditioned by our heredity and our environment, most obviously by the way we make our living and its adequacy to our needs. We are not totally determined by these conditioning factors. There is in human affairs an area of the unpredictable; that is, an area in which men have some freedom of choice to shape history. And to appeal to that freedom is not illusory. I cannot, therefore, accept a rigid economic determinism nor any other determinism in history or present-day politics. The approach to peace must be through economics and politics and ethics.

Vital as is the economic factor making for war or peace, the hopes many of us have had that national disputes could be bypassed by the offer of obviously desirable economic advantages has often been disappointed. Cyprus as a British base untorn by factional strife would be better off, not worse, economically, than partitioned between Greeks and Turks or united to Greece. Germaine Tillion (in her remarkable book, *Algeria, The Realities*, Knopf) makes a convincing case that the right sort of economic and political relations—such as have not existed—between France and Algeria would be better for the people than absolute Algerian independence. She has not as yet persuaded the independence movement or the French.

A committee centered around the distinguished scholar, historian, and advocate of peace, Boris Gourevitch, prepared an economic plan greatly to the advantage of all the peoples of the Middle East. It was prefaced by an eloquent history of good relations between Arabs and Jews in the Arabian Golden Age. All of it was translated into Arabic. I was asked to take some bilingual copies to the Middle East and see if they aroused any Arab support. I did, and while my efforts were necessarily rather superficial, I found no Arab interest in cooperating on the plan. Several Arabs told me that the history only made more inexcusable the Israeli intrusion on them! The Middle Eastern problem cannot be solved solely by an economic plan.

But neither can it be solved without one. That is notably true in the Arab lands because of the oil problem. But everywhere there must be an economic as well as a political approach to peace. Within nations that program must be consciously directed to provision for capital improvements and industrialization, not for the benefit of a small owning class or the "new class" of Communist totalitarianism, but for the people. Such a program must come to grips with the curse of a landlordism which makes virtual serfs out of the peasantry and with the dreadful incubus of overpopulation in many lands—Egypt, for instance, where food, schools, and the necessities for a good life must every year be provided for 500,000 more Egyptians in an area in which today there can be no expansion of cultivatable land. Even a high dam at Aswan, having become a reality, could only somewhat alleviate, not solve, the problem. As it is, the desperate desire for the available waters of the Nile tends to poison relations between Egypt and Sudan.

Here and in a great many other areas hope must lie in industrialization—and, too, in the perfecting of cheap methods to desalinize sea water and pump it onto parched lands. Hope must also lie in the spread of planned parenthood. The man or men who would perfect a workable plan for turning desalinized water onto desert land and give us safe orally administered contraceptives would bless mankind more effectually than the conquerors of space.

Neither the United States nor the United Nations can or should do all that must be done inside underdeveloped nations. Only their own peoples can do that. But the big Powers must recognize the right to revolution and refrain from becoming the allies of tyrants by reason of their economic interests or their ill-guided desire to win the cold war.

Some of the anti-American feeling around the world arises from the belief that our government is violating the principle we have set forth. Some of it arises from expectations of the impossible. Some of it from what it is easy to dub the jealousy of some nations against others allegedly getting more of our bounty; some from sheer resentment at our own wealth and power. Before we grow self-righteous in condemning that resentment it would be well to reflect on what a high Indian official told a group of us who were complaining against what we considered unjust criticisms of our country. "No one," said he, "living in a palace at the top of the hill can expect love from the dwell-

ers in huts at its foot even if he occasionally offers them
gifts."

Unquestionably most of the strength of Communism
in Asia is derived less from acceptance of its whole doctrine or practice, less from hope of any offer of immediate
utopia, than from the belief that Communism was the
power that built Russia, and more notably China, from
weakness to strength.

Twice in India in 1951 in cities far apart I was told
in almost the same words: "Mr. Thomas, we don't want to
be Communists, but we fear that only Communism can
discipline us for industrialization and make us tighten our
belts to derive capital from already hungry stomachs." It
is imperative that we help India find a better way. Walter
Lippmann is right that our best hope of containing Communism in Asia and Africa is to help India under social
democracy to build a healthy economy for her own people. Our eloquent but negative descriptions of Communism, although they contain much truth, will avail little,
especially in continents in which through millennia of time
there has been little or no tradition of civil liberty and
democracy as we understand them. Therefore there is less
concern for that of which Communist totalitarianism would
deprive them. And hence the necessity for us to help them
develop a program for their economic progress without
Communism.

The ruling passion of divisive sovereign nationalisms
has repeatedly run counter to the sound economic interests of the peoples concerned. If mankind is to enjoy peace
and plenty the nationalist obsession must yield to greater

cooperation in the UN and in regional federations. It was, for example, greatly to the economic disadvantage of the people that the Austro-Hungarian empire was succeeded by the succession states, each with its army, its tariffs, and its bureaucratic national establishments instead of by a greater Switzerland of closely federated cantons. The peoples paid in unnecessary poverty. Aside from the costly national strife which attended the partition of India, both India and Pakistan were weakened economically by the division of what had been a great free-trade area. It is, as we have noted, an added irritant to the tangle of troubles in the Middle East that the tiny sheikdoms of Kuwait and Bahrein should be regarded as sole owners and Arabian beneficiaries of the petroleum which the British concession-holders exploit.

One economic prerequisite of peace is freer movement of men and goods between nations. True international fraternity cannot flourish between nations boxed in by passport and travel restrictions, tariffs, harassing quota systems on exports and imports and multifarious currency controls. I do not suppose that absolute free trade such as so fortunately exists between the states of our American federal union is possible in a world of such unevenly developed national economies as ours, in which each nation is doing some planning on its own. That planning is inconsistent with a complete laissez-faire economy in international trade. The economies of countries producing minerals or such products as sugar and coffee may need the stabilizing influence of agreed quotas and prices as protection against the great fluctuations in price to which immediate supply and demand subject them, to the great hurt, for instance, of countries like Bolivia and Peru, largely dependent on the export from their mines.

But freer trade is essential, and at the American end the right of the President under specified conditions to make reciprocal trade agreements reducing tariffs is an excellent approach to it. The impact of the American economy upon the world is enormous. We produce 35 per cent of the world's goods and services. Our exports and imports constitute 16 per cent of the world's trade. If Congress had to choose (it didn't) between extension of the Reciprocal Trade Agreement and more adequate appropriations for economic aid, it probably was wise in voting for the former. But that law could be improved in its substance and in the way it has been administered.

At this point, however, one must give credit to the Eisenhower administration for changes for the better in its international economic policy. Edwin L. Dale, Jr., writing in the New York *Times* (Aug. 31, 1958), thus lists some of the things that have been done in a year.

"(1) After half a decade of talk, the United States has suddenly let the world know that it favors larger contributions, including dollar contributions, to the World Bank and Fund. These two institutions, particularly the fund, have played an extremely important role over the past few years in keeping the world economy on an even keel.

"(2) After an even longer period of talk, the United States has announced its willingness to consider contributing funds to an inter-American development bank. . . .

"(3) The staid old Export-Import Bank has quietly been converted into a major instrument for spot—and, in banking terms, rather 'unsound'—help for crisis situations in key countries. In the past year the bank has 'bailed out' or helped bail out Brazil, Colombia, Britain, the Philippines, Chile, and India. That is, it has sometimes made 'balance of payments' loans—loans direct to the treasury of a country that was desperate for foreign exchange—as distinct from carefully worked out 'project' loans for development. In some of these cases, the prospects for repayment are not all that a banker would like, though the bank will undoubtedly be repaid in the end. Also, an unpublicized new device has been discovered for helping to deal with these highly important balance-of-payments crises, namely, postponement of repayments due the United States on past loans. This has been used in the case of Britain, France, and Turkey.

"(4) The United States for the first time has announced its willingness to talk over the perennial request of the underdeveloped raw-material producing countries for 'commodity agreements' aimed at stabilizing prices and markets and thus stabilizing these nations' earnings of foreign exchange, possibly by some form of guaranteed minimum purchases by the U. S. The first item being discussed is coffee. Though in the end no agreement may be reached, the very participation of the U. S. in the discussions is something new under the sun.

"(5) The Administration swallowed its principles and recommended a subsidy and stockpiling scheme for the domestic mining industry rather than raise tariffs on lead, zinc, and possibly copper. The reason: the economic impact of higher tariffs on such key friends as Chile, Peru, and Mexico."

These progressive changes Mr. Dale attributes mostly to C. Douglas Dillon, banker, politician, and now Under Secretary of State for Economic Affairs. Unfortunately for Mr. Dale's rosy picture, part of the gains from this new policy were lost by the imposition of quotas on lead and zinc. On October 21, 1958, according to a report in the New York *Herald-Tribune*, Pedro Beltun, editor of *La Prensa*, in Lima, Peru, told the New York Economics Club that the imposition of these quotas had an effect "not softened in the least" by anything said at the meeting of foreign ministers and their "beautifully worded communiqué" shortly thereafter.

Two things are apparent from contemplation of this record of the Administration's progress: one, that it is obviously inadequate to the magnitude of the need and our resources for meeting it; the other, that it is guided by no comprehensive plan but is pragmatically eclectic. The Administration is very properly using UN agencies (the World Bank and Fund) and its own facilities while it also explores action through regional American agreements and a regional development bank. There is not now nor will there be in any near future a rigid rule or formula to determine the proportions of American aid by loan, gift, and

technical assistance which should be given through bilateral agreements, regional associations, and United Nations facilities. But there should be a more forthright fac-
ing of the problem.

So long as aid is considered as in some sense a weapon
in the cold war the American tendency will be so to apply it directly as to win for the United States the friendship and if possible the military support of the beneficiary
nation. Sometimes, as in aid to Tito's Yugoslavia, the best
the government can hope is to keep the nation out of the
economic and political clutches of the Soviet Union. Our
government has had enough good sense as well as humanity to aid India without expecting to break down her neutrality. In short, while neither the United States—nor, it
should be observed, the Soviet Union—can surely buy
political support by economic aid, each great Power still
hopes to win by its direct loans or gifts what it thinks
that it could not win if the same amount of money or technical service were given through a United Nations agency.

There are other reasons advanced for aid through bilateral agreements rather than through a UN authority.
Some American workers in the field have told me that it is
easier to administer than under conditions which the UN
with its cosmopolitan staff and controls must impose. Another is that the UN has such trouble raising its budget
for various worthy enterprises depending upon the willingness of the nations to contribute, and since the United
States always has to be the largest contributor, it can often
save time and trouble by acting on its own. I doubt if the
record supports this opinion.

Here, I think, the fundamental principle should be this: Since the best help is the help that enables the recipients to help themselves, the cooperative aspects of every program are of primary importance. We are not or should not be buying governments by doles, but aiding specific projects for development in which the maximum efforts of those to be benefited are enlisted. In many cases large sums of capital must be invested to get any start at the facilities, roads, means of communication, machinery on which healthy industrial development will depend. I once heard a spokesman of a great American bank explain to the visiting premier of an industrially underdeveloped country why he could not expect to get private capital to invest in his country's industrial development except perhaps in extractive industries: oil wells, mines for copper, zinc, tin, etc. No investment company could guarantee to private individuals a probable and safe return on their money, not, at any rate, until much preliminary work had been done to provide roads, schools, and the like.

In this field, like it or not, we all have to be socialists. The original supply of capital to a high degree must be provided on terms that cannot make it economically desirable for individual investors, but socially desirable for us all in terms of human progress in peace and the conquest of poverty. It is surely better that this provision should be made as far as possible by a great association of nations in cooperation to one of their number in need of help rather than by a rich nation to a poor, dependent people. Better, that is, if the cooperative idea can be worked out so that every nation contributes, no matter how little, to the common development authority. India and the Arab nations are very poor, but they have some very rich men who should be appropriately taxed for any world development fund. All this points to the UN as the ideal agency for establishing a World Development Authority, provided a plan can be worked out for financing it more adequately and equitably than has been the case in most UN enterprises.

This whole matter of world development and its support is, like so many other problems, carefully examined and dealt with by Messrs. Clark and Sohn in *World Peace through World Law*. I quote certain paragraphs setting forth their concept of a World Economic Development Authority and its relation to the organs of the UN.

The Authority's "function would be to assist in the economic and social development of the underdeveloped areas of the world, primarily through grants-in-aid and interest-free loans. This Authority would be under the direction of a World Development Commission of five members to be chosen with due regard to geographical distribution by the Economic and Social Council, subject to confirmation by the General Assembly.

"The World Development Commission would be under the general supervision of the Economic and Social Council which would have power to define broad objectives and priorities. That Council would be composed of twenty-four Representatives of whom twelve would come from the member Nations with the highest gross national products and twelve from the other member Nations. Assurance would thus be provided that proper account would be taken not only of the views of those nations contributing large shares of United Nations revenue, but also of the nations most in need of the Authority's assistance.

"This proposed World Development Authority could, if the General Assembly so decided, have very large sums at its disposal, since the Authority's funds would be allocated to it by the Assembly out of the general revenues of the United Nations. With the large resources which the Assembly could and should provide, the World Development Authority would have the means to aid the underdeveloped areas of the world to the extent necessary to remove the danger to peace caused by the immense economic disparty between those areas and the industrialized regions of the world."

And this is their proposal for financing the UN and through it the Authority:

"A chief feature of this system would be that each member Nation would assign in advance to the United Nations all or part of certain designated taxes assessed under its national laws. Each nation would undertake the entire administrative function of collecting the taxes thus assigned to the United Nations, these taxes to be paid directly to a fiscal office of the United Nations in each member Nation. In this way it would be unnecessary to create any considerable United Nations bureaucracy for this purpose.

"Another important feature would be an *over-all limit* on the maximum amount of revenue to be raised in any year, namely two per cent of the gross world product (total value of all goods produced and services rendered) as estimated from year to year by the above-mentioned permanent committee of the General Assembly (the Standing Committee on Budget and Finance)."

I have not quoted these paragraphs as the final word on the subject but as a rational, concrete proposal for discussion and action, action not to be postponed indefinitely when one considers the urgency of the problem and Gunnar Myrdal's warning of the widening gap.

My own inclination is to emphasize rather more than Messrs. Clark and Sohn have done the value of regional economic organization; certainly in Europe, certainly in other continents, although not necessarily under the same formula. We have already seen its necessity in the economy of the Middle East and in dealing with its riches in oil.

The emergence of a flock of new nations in Africa will emphasize the importance of regional federations in that continent. Each of these nations south of the Sahara, whose ruling groups are passionately nationalist, is more or less artificial, containing tribes not bound together by language or native history but held within boundaries imposed by the old rivalries of colonial powers, and united in so far as they are united by desire for freedom from those powers. Their new rulers are likely to load their people down with armies as badges of nationhood and tie in their emerging economies with all sorts of nationalist restrictions. Many of their political difficulties and their economic interests can be better handled by regional federations than if there is nothing between them and the UN.

Here in the Western Hemisphere I was very much taken by the bold suggestions in the Rockefeller panel report, *Foreign Economic Policy for the Twentieth Century,* for cooperative action by all the nations of the Western Hemisphere including Canada. Such an Inter-American Conference could do in the whole field of economics what the UN cannot in any near future. Rather surprisingly the Report does not discuss specifically the role of the UN. It does say, very wisely, that the regional arrangements its authors recommend "do not imply regional autarky. Their aim is the progressive elimination of barriers within groups, not the erection of new barriers between groups." That is a sentiment which will not work itself out automatically. A sound economy for the twentieth century will require statesmanlike correlation of national economy with both regional and worldwide economic organization. It cannot be purely national.

Not even the United States is strong enough to stand alone economically. Its prosperity and its peace will not very long permit it to be an affluent society in a poverty-stricken world. Cooperation in a holy war against this technologically unnecessary poverty is a spiritual necessity in a world where even the most amply provided cannot live by bread alone. It is also essential to the endurance of our own prosperity and peace. The United States has been generous. Its generosity must be continued and more wisely guided. Its motive must not be merely the necessity to meet Communist competition for the favor of Asian or African peoples. (But we can learn something from our rivals in these lands who, we are told, do not live in "golden ghettoes" as the people of Asia have been known to refer to the local American colonies.) Since cooperation is essential to achieve the plenty so important to worldwide peace and fraternity, the agencies of the UN and of regional federations should be progressively used in economic aid rather than bilateral agreements between a rich Uncle Sam and his poor relations.

XII.

The Dynamics of Peace

THIS BOOK has been written in the faith that there are prerequisites for peace in themselves thoroughly rational and not beyond the acceptance of men and nations most of whom are obviously unready to embrace the Sermon on the Mount as their guide in politics or accept Gandhi's noble nonviolent resistance to evil as the alternative to war. Our America is far more likely to disarm from military strength than from weakness. It will demand that its disarmament be part of a multilateral project, not an effort to lead men in a confused world by one outstanding idealistic act. To work for such disarmament is anything but utopian.

Yet as I have written I have been increasingly troubled about the dynamics of peace. Men want it; they recoil with horror from the thought of nuclear war. Yet, from times before the dawn of history, war has been part of the life pattern of tribes, nations, and empires. Men have cherished what they hate. Today smaller nations may want renunciation of nuclear war by the strong, but they cling to their own military forces and the trappings of war as proof and protection of their sovereignty. In all nations, great and small, important groups and classes have a stake, if not in war then in the preparation for it which historically has led to it rather than to peace. In military preparedness soldiers and civilians find sources of power, prestige, and profit. These facts alone would explain why we cannot rely on the growing understanding and fear of nuclear war by itself to keep the peace.

But there is more. For many men there is a terrible fascination in the weapons of death which science is giving us. For example, on the Sunday before Labor Day 1958, *Parade*, a Sunday magazine widely circulated by newspapers, carried as its frontispiece an exciting picture of an airplane, F105B, "the world's deadliest one-man weapon," 69,000 parts to make The Beast, as its handlers fondly call it. The descriptive article is of a sort consciously or unconsciously to stimulate in an active young man a desire to try it. Very high officials in our own United States before a Congressional Committee have dwelt almost lovingly on their calculation of what our arms might do should we establish superiority in space (See Chapter II). Khrushchev has been trying to assure the world that only Americans even think of surprise attack as a road to victory. But on March 24, 1955, his Marshall Romistrov wrote: "In some cases surprise aggression might become a deciding condition of success not only in the initial phases of war but even in its final outcome." Six weeks later General Kornichenko added: "The importance of the surprise factor in contemporary war has increased tremendously." (Quoted by C. L. Sulzberger in the New York *Times*, November 10, 1958.) A mere balance of terror will not indefinitely restrain men in powerful position on both sides who think like that. The nations will not be safe until consciously, under effective sanctions, they renounce the arms race. And that will require stronger dynamics than mere emotional horror of the new kind of war in the nuclear age.

That emotional horror might be more easily made the inspiration of a program for peace were it not for two facts. The first is the fixed idea on both sides of the cold war that sooner or later what the enemy claims is for his defense will be used by him for aggression. To this controlled disarmament is the obvious answer for both sides, since each claims to want peace, not aggression. Understanding of that fact is vital to the dynamics of peace.

Here we are confronted with a second fact. In a democracy like our own it is very difficult to get a sustained and intelligent appreciation of or interest in the processes of disarmament and disengagement on which war or peace depend. Usually men have awakened to the peril of war after it is too late to avert it. Hatred of nuclear war cannot prevent it if the public has been nurtured on indiscriminate hatred and suspicion of the enemy and caught in the sort of policy that suspicion dictates. In the United States our mixed emotions of hatred of Communism and opposition to World War III have gone along with widespread apathy about the concrete actions of the government, on which the issue of total war may depend.

James Reston—also on the Sunday before Labor Day —began his influential column in the New York *Times* by discussing American interest in racial integration *vs.* segregation in our schools. (Our racial problem also has an effect on our leadership for peace.) Then Mr. Reston continued:

"This [integration] is not like other historic issues now before the nation. Public indifference seems to be the rule of the day on other questions. Secretary of State Dulles committed the United States to defend nations right up against the southern border of the Soviet Union, without a word of protest from anybody. President Eisenhower sent the Marines to Lebanon and there was very little complaint.

"Even this week, the President dispatched more aircraft carriers to the Formosa Strait and the Administration indicated that it was ready to help repel a Chinese Communist invasion of Quemoy, within slingshot distance of the China coast. In the process, the President said he was not sure whether United States commanders were or were not authorized to use atomic weapons in defense of their command. And all this passed without a public murmur."

Later, as we have seen, there was a considerable awakening to events in the Formosa Strait. Probably some degree of apprehension over our policy had its effect on Mr. Dulles himself and later on the Congressional election. But, on the whole, popular apathy on foreign policy continues, interrupted only now and then by alarm over the danger of nuclear tests. To stop the tests, important as such a step would be, could not of itself alone be a barrier to a third world war. A persistent pursuit of a positive peace must be added to the emotional reaction against H-bombs to win us a true security.

Nevertheless, despite all difficulties, I am persuaded that the world is sufficiently aware of the fact that nuclear war can mean annihilation to respond powerfully to effective leadership for peace. Such leadership is conspicuously lacking throughout the world. Our President might have supplied it. Mr. Eisenhower is a man of high intentions and has a real concern for peace. He has held a high place in men's opinion. But he came to office inexpert and untrained in political matters. He has had a passive conception of the presidency and is prone to delay decisions and action until events are upon him. Hence his failure to do what might earlier have been done for American race relations at home and American honor abroad in the matter of school integration. Hence his handling of the Quemoys, which ought to have been evacuated by Chiang's forces before they became an issue which might set off World War III. Mr. Eisenhower has accomplished some good things for peace but it is not difficult to imagine what he might have accomplished had he a more forceful conception of his office, an intelligent long-range peace program, a very different Secretary of State, and something like Roosevelt's genius for fireside chats.

No nation in the non-Communist world is supplying such desperately needed leadership. The United States, because she is the strongest of non-Communist nations is the most derelict. One reason for this failure is the ruling passion of nationalism. No leader of his nation dares to say to his people—and mean it—"above all nations is humanity." Men live by their loyalties, and nationalism has a high and legitimate place in their loyalties, provided that it does not become the ultimate loyalty. Nationalism as a principle of self-government against imperialism is to be honored, but not nationalism which deifies the nation-state until power is the only ethic in its conduct.

That brings us back to an inquiry into what potential forces there are in the United States which can develop a dynamics of peace and with it the indispensable leadership we have lacked. There is a widespread interest in the UN. There are valuable organizations of various sorts dealing with one aspect or another of the problems of peace —the World Federalists, the American Association for the United Nations, and the Foreign Policy Association, to name a few.

More organic in our society are the strong organizations, religious and labor, which have international connections and some real concern for peace. Organized socialism, weak in America, is such a force in the world. I have mourned the chance it lost in 1914. But today, when in much of the world socialism is the only viable alternative to Communism, the Socialist International is a real force for peace—this despite the French Socialists' performance in Algeria and the truth expressed by Paul-Henri Spaak when he said, "The thing that Socialists have learned best how to nationalize is socialism." It must not be forgotten that it was the socialist British Labour Party which pioneered, beginning in India, in the friendly liquidation of empire.

On the international scene the Confederation of Free Trade Unions to which the powerful AFL-CIO belongs is making some genuine contribution to international justice and friendship and hence to peace.

But here, as in the nation, much depends on leadership and its zeal for educational work among the masses. There is, alas, in the "plain people" or the workers no such zeal for universal brotherhood and abiding peace as some great idealists have believed was instinctive. If one may borrow theological language, the love for a fraternity crossing racial and national lines is a state of grace to which most of us in every walk of life have to be converted or persuaded.

That is true in the great religious organizations. In America today the churches have this in common with organized labor: their official statements (which could be improved) are almost always better than the performance of the mass of their members. In both cases the ideals of labor and of the religious organizations have inspired individuals to outstanding acts of service. But scarcely the organizations as a whole. The American churches in World War I went crazy beating the drums for war and gave their conscientious objectors short shrift. This was in line with the tradition which has made most Christian churches anything but pacifist organizations ever since the time of Constantine. More often than not religious fervor has given drive and sanction to bigotry. Sir Harry Lauder, the pop-

ular Scotch singer and comedian, put it this way in World
War I: "God told us to forgive our enemies, but not His.
The Germans are His enemies."

In recent years the American churches, Protestant and
Catholic, have improved in relation to the approach to
peace and even more markedly to racial integration. They
still have a long way to go. At the moment the leaders are
ahead of the rank and file, whom they are more diligently
seeking to lead in achieving world peace than in years
gone by. Few American churchmen would be as sure as
His Grace of Canterbury that it may be God's providence
that the race of men should perish by the weapons they
have made.

There is, I think, some hope that the next Congress
will have a more constructive influence on foreign policy
than its recent predecessors. All Congresses, however, are
subject to certain strong group pressures. Congress, even
more than the executive, is affected by the especial interest taken by large immigrant groups in the passions, politics, and interests of the countries from which they or
their fathers came: Ireland, Poland, Italy, etc. With the
decline of immigration that influence (which scarcely
made for secure international peace) has, I think, lessened
considerably. It is still true, however, that a New York
City politician does well to make the holy "three-I pil-
grimage" to Ireland, Italy, and Israel, bearing gifts, if he
wishes votes at home. Exiles naturally, have added passion to this hyphenated feeling. A distinguished Polish
exile now resident in Britain after a tour on which he addressed a great many Polish-American clubs told me his

worry. It was that as a matter of course they expected a war of liberation fought by America for the captive nations, whereas he knew that the Polish people had a better understanding of the new sort of war and wanted "something liberated in Poland besides their graves."

Quite understandably the strongest bloc of this sort in America is Zionist or at least strongly pro-Israeli. A congressman told me with, I suspect, some exaggeration, that none of his Eastern colleagues would dare vote on any question closely affecting Israel contrary to the well-propagandized Israeli position. That is an additional reason why a settlement of the Arab-Israeli dispute is so important for peace.

When all is said and done, public opinion is a mysterious thing, not wholly made by the mass media and the Madison Avenue boys in the service of a dominant elite. None of us is so inconspicuous that his concern for peace need be of no account. Each man beginning with himself can help the growth of mutual understanding between peoples. And that understanding is basic to any effort of governmental leaders to secure working agreements rather than propaganda advantage. The growing exchanges of visitors: students, savants, athletes, and artists, farmers and workers and businessmen—all will help to create a better atmosphere for constructive negotiation.

But useful as better acquaintance may be, it is not of itself a great dynamic of peace to nations caught in the cold war. If mankind is not to perish, there must be on men's part a moral, economic, and political approach to world peace.

The great interest aroused in Britain by George Kennan's speeches over the British Broadcasting System showed that at least to atomic war there is a moral response transcending mere negative fear. Writing along the line of his speeches in *Harper's Magazine* (February 1958), Mr. Kennan made this moving statement:

"The technological realities of this competition are constantly changing from month to month and from year to year. Are we to flee like haunted creatures from one defensive device to another, each more costly and humiliating than the one before, cowering underground one day, breaking up our cities the next, attempting to surround ourselves with elaborate electronic shields on the third, concerned only to prolong the length of our lives while sacrificing all the values for which it might be worthwhile to live at all? If I thought that this was the best the future held for us, I should be tempted to join those who say, 'Let us divest ourselves of this weapon altogether; let us stake our safety on God's grace and our own good consciences and on that measure of common sense and humanity which even our adversaries possess; but then let us at least walk like men, with our heads up, so long as we are permitted to walk at all.'"

It is to me somewhat surprising that a man who could write this passage should be so lukewarm on disarmament. Or so inclined to confine his ethics to wars fought with nuclear weapons. There are other weapons of mass destruction.

The Second World War was fought against the hideous evil of Nazism. But to the rank and file at the front it was, as described by Lester Atwell, for instance, in his vivid book, *Private,* something rather different than a moral crusade. Now a better way must be found if our race is to endure. It is war as it was in 1945 as well as war as it may be in 1965 which must be eliminated. That elimination will require, as this book has been arguing, far more than a holy hatred of war. Yet that hatred is essential to the dynamics of peace.